HELL HAS NO STARS

JUSTIN A. MERCER

CONTENTS

Foreword

Dedication

Acknowledgements

More About The Author

FOREWORD

This story is a work of non-fiction. As such, the only name mentioned is my own. There are many real people that play a role in this story: for better or worse. I have chosen to leave all names out of it. I did not write this to put blame on anyone. I did not write this to complain. I wrote this book because I hope that by sharing my story that I can possibly help at least one person by showing them that they are not alone.

DEDICATION

This one is for my family. Thank you for supporting me in everything I do. This is also for my friends, thanks for standing by me when I need you. Most importantly this book is for all the men, women and families struggling with any mental illness, depression, and suicide. You are not alone.

Justin A. Mercer

CHAPTER 1
INTRODUCTIONS

Well hi there. As you can see from the cover of the book my name is Justin A. Mercer, the "A" stands for Allen. So as you can guess from the title and genre, this is a book about mental health, more specifically, my mental health.

Now I don't want to mislead any of you, I am not a licensed psychologist; I don't even have a degree. Although I am in college, I am not even studying psychology. I am studying history because I want to be a history teacher. That is my passion, but more on that later. I am simply a person wanting to share my experience in the hope of it possibly helping someone else.

This book is not a solution manual. This book is not meant to hand out a diagnosis. I wrote this book simply to tell my story in hopes that others stuck in the same struggle I am can see that fighting back against depression and mental illness is possible. I wrote this book so that society can see that people with mental issues are not inhumane monsters that they are sometimes portrayed to be. I wrote this book so that people that do not struggle with depression can hopefully gain an understanding of how it feels, so that we can adjust how we handle people with any mental illness. I can only speak from the viewpoint of a depressed person. I do not know everything; I do not have all the answers. This is just my attempt to use a bad experience that I have had to help make the world a better place.

CHAPTER 2
MORE ABOUT ME

Now some more about me; just to give you an accurate picture of who I am, trust me, it's important for the story. I'm a history geek. I can tell you almost everything and more than you wanted to know about anything historical. I actually enjoy taking history tests if that tells you anything. I also fall into the category of "nerd". I've seen almost every episode of "Star Trek." My favorite movie is Star Wars Episode IV: A New Hope. My favorite video games are the Elder Scrolls series; Skyrim would have to be my favorite of the series. Of course the classics like Mario Kart and Super Smash Bros. are great for hanging out with people.

So, if most of you reading this want to stop right now because you are imagining a dorky nerd sitting at his computer and writing this, well you wouldn't be wrong. Indulge me a little and let me continue on, I promise this will all be important later. Usually everything about characters in a book are revealed through time, but this isn't a story book in the traditional sense I thought it would make more sense to introduce myself completely now. Moving on.

I drive an F150. I love my truck. I also ride a Kawasaki Ninja 500. I love my motorcycle and it was the first big thing I've ever purchased using entirely my own money. I am quite proud of my bike. I go shooting with my Dad as often as possible. While I do enjoy rifle shooting, I have always been a good shot with a pistol. Personally I use a Smith and Wesson M&P 9. I love the outdoors, on a nice day you can often find me in a hammock somewhere. I love camping. I love hiking. I love whitewater rafting. I am also an Eagle Scout. I am an avid reader. I've read all the basics, Harry Potter, Game of Thrones, The Hunger Games, and I've also read tons of other books. While my favorite modern series would have to be Game of Thrones like everyone else, one of my all-time favorite books is The Inferno by Dante Alighieri. Yes, one of my all-time favorites is a classic piece of Italian literature.

I am a Brother in the National Service Fraternity Alpha Phi Omega. I am a Brother of Delta Chapter at Auburn University.

I have a tattoo on my left shoulder commemorating my membership. Yes, it is a "frat tat" no, I do not regret it. I joined a service fraternity, so I clearly enjoy helping people. I go on mission trips to Honduras with my family almost every year. I am not religious though. In fact I would consider myself agnostic. Actually, I just don't think about the whole religion question that much. I don't even think about it enough to decide if I believe in a higher power or not. Religion just isn't important to me at this point in my life, but trust me, I have my reasons. Regardless, I do enjoy helping people. I think it is just a human desire and doesn't need to be associated with religion.

As far as athletics go, I attempt to go to the gym or running at least three times a week. Though that very rarely happens… I run whenever I am guilted into it. I was Cross Country team captain in high school, but I don't particularly enjoy running. I love soccer. I love playing it and I love watching it. My favorite team is Manchester United, and no I am not a bandwagon fan. My grandparents are from Manchester and got me hooked early in my life. My favorite player would have to be Zlatan Ibrahimović. I liked him at Milan and PSG. When he transferred to United and I saw more about him he cemented his place at the top of the list. (Sorry Cristiano Ronaldo, if I had a draft of all players I would pick you on my team before Zlatan, but you're second in my favorite players book). I like Ronaldo and Zlatan because of their ample self-confidence, and how they back it up by being among the world's best. Maybe it is because they are everything that I want to be that I like them so much. Sadly, I did not play soccer in high school, more on that later. I was born in Georgia. I live in Alabama, and I attend Auburn University. Of course, I love college football. War Damn Eagle.

As far as music goes I listen to almost everything. I know everyone says that, but I am actually serious. On my iPhone you can find choral and orchestral music, Broadway music, heavy metal, and even rap. I am a sucker for most classic rock songs and it is what my parents raised me on. I even enjoy the occasional country song, though it is not my favorite genre. If you ever have the misfortune of riding in a car with me you may hear me go from badly rapping Eminem's "Not Afraid" to badly singing parts of "Red and Black" from *Les*

Miserables.

So as you can see, I am a rather eclectic person. When I write it out like this, I don't think I would mind hanging out with that person. So what is wrong with my life? It seems fairly normal and not bad without any apparent tragedies. So why am I writing this book?

Well, I am writing this book because for the longest time I have not been able to enjoy my life. I still find it hard to enjoy my life. If possible, I want to help others not to have the same experience that I have had. The only way I know how to do this is by telling my story.

Now for the longest time I assumed that was just how life was, that life was just kind of "blah" for everyone. Then as my life progressively became worse, in my eyes, I realized that no; it was just me. I was the only one who experienced this on a daily basis. That realization caused my world view to sink even further into despair. It wasn't until the spring of 2013 that I was officially diagnosed with depression.

Now let's go back to the beginning. What better place to start a journey? It has been a journey through hell for me, my own personal hell. Trapped within my own mind, I have delved into the very coldest depths of hell. I am my own Dante. Sadly, I did not have a Virgil to guide me through my own personal hell.

While writing this book will help me in my recovery, my ultimate hope is that by sharing my story I can help someone else. It doesn't matter to me who it is; a parent of a kid having similar issues to me, or a kid that recognizes they might be having problems and ask for help. This for sure will help me, and I can only hope it will help at least one person. Maybe I can show people that there are Virgil's out there, and that this is a fight that they are not alone in. That maybe they can find someone to help them through hell.

Writing this is hard for me, and if you are going through what I am, it may be hard for you to read. I have to face my demons here in putting all of this on paper for the entire world to see; maybe this will help you face yours.

Justin A. Mercer

CHAPTER 3
A TRIP BACK TO THE BEGINNING

6th grade was an interesting year in my life. I was a Montessori school in a small town outside of Birmingham, Alabama. The school was really small, and most of my 7 classmates were leaving to go to other schools. Had I stayed, I would have been the only student in 7th grade. I did not want to be the only student in my grade. So, I had two choices, go to the local public school for a year, or attempt to skip a grade and go on to a local private school. The private school is one of the most prestigious private schools in Alabama and it runs from 8th grade through 12th grade.

Rather than be the new kid for two years in a row, my parents and I decided that it would be a good idea to go ahead and skip 7th grade. I had passed all the entrance exams, and Indian Springs accepted me. Indian Springs runs from 8th through 12th grade. I was on my way to high school and I was not even a teenager yet. I would turn 13 in November of my 8th grade year.

From the start, I didn't really fit in. I was small, as I had not yet hit puberty. I was also incredibly self-conscious as most young almost teenagers are. I started the year wearing glasses and was terrified of being called "four eyes". Acne had come before my growth spurt, and when I did finally grow, I was awkward. I hadn't yet grown into my relatively tall frame. Not to mention, I was a year younger and had come from a class of eight people; seven guys and one girl. I had almost no social experience, and yet here I was; high school. Unlike in the movies, the awkward new kid doesn't show up and instantly become friends with one of the cool kids and they don't sing and dance their way through hallways. It just doesn't work that way.

Already the odds were stacked against me. What followed would be a deadly cocktail of events that would take my natural social anxiety and throw me down a dark path that would define me for the years to come.

My 8th grade class had 25 people, and really, I did not fit in with any of them. Most of them came from incredibly affluent families and had known each other for years before coming here.

At this time, my Dad owned his own company. While that sounds great, it wasn't. This was 2007-2008. My Dad's company dealt heavily in the auto industry. While at this time we were doing pretty well, I was still not born with a silver spoon in my mouth. My Dad had worked for everything we had, I was proud of him. His company was doing well; I loved the fact that our family name was on shirts and jackets. It made me feel like one of those affluent kids to be able to say "my Dad owns his own company."

So not only was my family in a different tax bracket than most families at this private school, I was a small, acne faced, and four eyed twelve year old. I was automatically disqualified from the "cool" crowd. I wasn't from the right part of town, didn't attend the right church or synagogue, and didn't go to the right middle school. Oh, and I wasn't attractive and I was a self-professed nerd. My application for the "cool" crowd was clearly denied. The crowd I ended up joining… in retrospect, I would have been better off starting out alone.

The crowd I ended up joining was a group of cynical kids who were either trying to be rebels, or just trying to be jackasses because they thought it was cool. Before I knew it, I was the butt of all the jokes. Every time I was around, I was being made fun of. People do make fun of their friends, that much I understand. I do it still today, yet I always make sure I do it out of love and let them take equal shots back at me. At some point though I realized that my so called "friends" were not making fun of me out of love. If I ever tried to return fire with a zinger of my own, or participate in the roasting of someone else, everyone would turn on me and verbally gun me down. Welcome to high school I guess.

Even back then, I was self-driven, so I decided to do something about my torment. A common thing that I was made fun of for was the unhealthy dose of acne I seemed to have. I get it. Everyone gets a pimple now and then, but from what I remember, I had a lot of acne. Pretty much I was sick and tired of being made fun of for being ugly. I hated myself and especially hated my terrible self-image. So I decided to change it figuring that when I stopped having this physical defect that my tormenters would stop and we could go back to being friends. Yes, I was incredibly naïve…I was only thirteen.

I started with all of the usual acne medication; the creams, the wipes, that sort of thing. It wasn't working fast enough for me. I wanted results now. I had solved the four eyes problem, I was wearing contacts. If I only could get rid of this acne, maybe my "friends" would stop making fun of me and I could fit in better. I decided to take an anti-acne pill.

This pill was pretty much the nuclear bomb of anti-acne medication. If you think it sounds familiar, they were being sued for the side effects not long ago. I am not using the name on purpose. The side effects list was a literal booklet. My mom and I had to sign a contract agreeing we had read this booklet. The side effects were anything from kidney failure, depression, blinding headaches, and death. I had to get blood tested bi-weekly while on this to make sure my kidneys were not going to shut down. So I took it for a while, the acne mostly cleared up as was advertised, but I was still the butt of all jokes. I was still constantly made fun of for no better reason than I was the easiest target. My unhappiness became visible to my parents. Or more so the unhappiness coupled with the blinding headaches. The blinding headaches were incredibly annoying. I was taken off the drug. Problem solved. My negativity should have died with the blinding headaches. Or rather that is what my parents thought.

Time went on and I got sick and tired of being made fun of. I simply took to avoiding people. By people I mean everyone at school, even those who were kind of nice to me. I scurried from class to class. Yes, scurried. I scurried around as if I were a hunted animal. When I wasn't in class I would hide out in the back corner of the library, where I could be alone with books for sometimes hours on end after school. I think I was the only one who read most of those books. This wasn't weird for this private school though. We had the incredibly rich kids, and then we had the rather strange kids. It was a private school; I just happened to be that weird kid so no one thought anything of it.

I did though. In an attempt to rationalize my behavior of avoiding people I adopted terms that I had learned from a Tom Clancy book: The DEFCON system. DEFCON stands for Defense Condition; it is a Cold War term to describe how threatened the US was feeling by the Soviet Union. At

DEFCON 5, the United States was at peace. All military units were at peacetime condition. At DEFCON 1 we were pretty much at war with the Soviets and preparing to launch all of our nukes to turn Moscow into glass. At DEFCON 5 I had the lowest chance of being made fun of. At DEFCON 1…I was either about to be made fun of, or in the process of being made fun of. At school, I was usually at DEFCON 3 or 2. That translates to massive social anxiety.

Yes, I was a weird kid. What other type of kid would even think of coming up with a system like I did with the DEFCONs? You could say I was going a little bit crazy. The constant scurrying around, looking down at my feet, I was doing my best not to be noticed. My attitude of not being noticed was even reflected in my wardrobe. I wore plain shirts. Not necessarily black, god forbid, I be noticed as an emo kid. Dark green, dark blue, I wore nothing bright, nothing with labels or logos on the front. No band t-shirts, nothing supporting my favorite football or soccer teams, and god forbid anything that might give away my political standpoint. I was doing my best to blend in to the pavement, yet I still was not happy. In fact, my constant living in fear made me even more unhappy. I guess I know what it feels like to be a hunted animal. I hated my high school. I wanted nothing more than to escape.

In truth, I hated myself too. When I imagined starting high school I did not imagine this. I obviously wasn't expecting it to be all happiness and sunshine, but I thought it would be better than this. I hated how I hid myself all day. I hated how I walked around afraid with my eyes downcast. I hated how I couldn't turn invisible and hide from everyone. I hated how the only people that took any notice of me were intent on making fun of me. I was a small kid, so it's not like I could physically stand up for myself. I was outnumbered and would have gotten my ass handed to me. Plus, fighting was not part of the culture of my high school; I didn't want to stand out anymore by causing one. No hero upperclassman came in to save the day. The biggest kid in my grade wasn't a kind hearted giant who took on the bullies for me. I couldn't help myself and no one would help me. I was alone. I was struggling. I couldn't handle it.

Eventually, I got fed up and had a breakdown. It was

midway through the first semester of my 9th grade year. My Mom and Dad confronted me about being negative and angry all the time and pestered me for reasons why I was like that. My response was not very convincing to them.

"I hate my school. I want to go to the public school so I can play football." Looking back I couldn't have said anything else more stupid than that. I would not have made the football team even if I had transferred. Yes, I can run fast, but I weighed about 120 pounds and stood about 5'9". I can catch a football about as well as any other American kid. My throwing was below average. I can run fast in a straight line, but I am not particularly agile. Maybe I could have been a kicker or punter, but I also had no experience kicking a football. Essentially, I would have been destroyed the first time I got hit if I even made the team, which I would not have.. My parents knew this. They knew I loved watching football and throwing it around at halftime with my Dad, but I had never before expressed a desire to play on a team. I had zero experience. So really, anything would have been a much better excuse.

My parents pushed and pushed for the true reason I wanted to abandon my education at one of the best private schools in Alabama, especially one that they were working so hard to pay for. I was sitting on the back deck of our house in a hammock chair that was my little sister's. Eventually, I broke down and started crying. I never cry. It's not a macho thing with me, I am secure in my manhood, I just don't cry. It is not something I do on any sort of regular basis. Finally, I blubbered out that I had been bullied almost constantly since starting school the last year. My parents refused to stand for it. They marched me in to the school administrators and demanded that something happen to stop me from being bullied. In the end the school suspended the kid most responsible for my torment. I didn't even want that to happen to him though. I just wanted him to stop. He did, but the next few weeks were quite uncomfortable as I was constantly questioned about why I would do such a thing in getting him suspended. I just could not win. While the main harassment had ended, I had only succeeded in alienating myself from everyone even more.

After winter break though, life sort of mellowed out. I still had this "negative vibe" about me, and was still constantly in a negative mood, but things were becoming more normal. I found a good group of friends that would stick with me throughout the rest of high school. At the time, I did not know that though. I went into summer still with the feelings of uncertainty, and naturally with feelings of anxiety. Those feelings were always around.

CHAPTER 4
TO BOLDLY GO

The summer between my 9th and 10th grade years I had a grand adventure. My granddad took me whitewater rafting for a week down the Colorado River through the Grand Canyon. To say that this was an amazing time is an understatement. I felt truly happy out there away from the world at the bottom of a canyon in the middle of the desert. I have always loved looking at stars, space, and astronomy. The stars at night were amazing. With no light pollution for miles and miles, the sky was littered with stars. My most vivid memory of the trip was on our first night in the canyon. An incredible desert thunderstorm had lit up the sky with lightning. In defiance of the windblown sandstorm, the driving rain, and the constant crack of thunder, I slept outside… I was channeling my true adventurer here. After about an hour or so of hiding under a tarp to escape the wind powered sand blasting that I was receiving, I was rewarded for my fortitude by one of the most beautiful sights I have ever seen. Considering this was at a time where life was constantly rather dim for me, this attests to the true beauty of the moment.

The storm was slackening up and moving on; as the rain stopped I peeked out from under my tarp and looked up at the sky. This thunderstorm that was the unbridled fury of nature was being pulled back like a curtain and disappearing from view past the top of the canyon wall. There I was staring up at the sky as this curtain was thrown back and the clearest of night skies became visible. I have never seen a sight more beautiful. A curtain of a thunderstorm, and the clearest night sky framed by millions of year old rock, and here was little "ole" me, viewing it from the bottom of this canyon next to a raging river. It was a very surreal moment, and one of the few I remember from this time as being truly happy.

Tenth grade year started and I was determined to hit "reset" and begin anew. In the space of a semester, I asked out three girls. All of them said no. I asked one to our school's Winter Formal. I asked her out and she didn't just say no, she avoided the dance entirely. Talk about a confidence booster…The start of sophomore year was interesting. I was still trying to solidify my friend group; I would be confused on this until junior year. I was doing ok in life, grades were good, and besides the average feeling of "blah" and the occasional crash of unhappiness I was doing alright. I was still worried that the bullying might start again, and besides being talked down to a little since I was the weird kid, it never really did.

It wasn't until after winter break that I thought my life was heading on the up and up. Second semester of 10th grade was an anomaly for me. For the first real time in my life, I was in a relationship. I actually managed to have a relationship with an actual girl, a human female. Wow.

Little did I know that relationships are hard, and for a person with my social anxiety and chronically negative disposition, they are even harder. Still, I gave it a good shot. I finally had my first kiss (cue the daww or bleh soundtrack, whichever suits your fancy) so I would be lying through my teeth if I told you that this relationship wasn't enjoyable

So, I had a pretty darn good semester by all accounts. I had friends, a girlfriend; I was doing things with them on weekends. I felt like almost like normal high schooler, I just needed to "stop being negative all the time". That was still a problem that haunted my daily existence. During this semester I decided to try something. I figured out that I could get sympathetic feelings from people by "accidentally" cutting myself with a knife or sword. Wait, did he just say sword? Yes, I have a sword or two...or five. I did fencing for a while, and I love military history. At this time I was slightly obsessed with warrior cultures so my parents bought me one of those katana sets that are really made in China out of aluminum. It made sense, I loved weapons and these were particularly good looking and I could tell you the real history of the Samurai and these swords. They looked cool, and while not Japanese folded steel, they were still blades. I accidentally cut part of my bedroom ceiling fan in half with one. That was a true accident. The fan hasn't spun right to this day.

So, with these weapons I discovered that by bleeding a little, I could get attention and sympathy from family, friends, and my girlfriend. It was not a common practice. In my lowest moments, when I felt alone and felt that people were 'ignoring' me, I would simply let a knife or sword slip. As a Boy Scout and soon to be Eagle Scout, I had a plethora of pocket knives. I found ways to make everything into an accident. I would make the knife slip while sharpening it. I would accidentally make a rash downward cut while playing around with my katana. A slice on the finger here, a cut on the leg there... Oddly enough it is only in hindsight that I realized why I did that. I never identified myself as a cutter or self-harmer, but my actions speak for me. I didn't wear exceptionally dark clothing, I did not wear white makeup with dark eyeliner, and at this time I even used an electric razor. I've not cut myself with a razor blade unless it was a legitimate shaving accident. I have cut my hands on purpose though, but one of my favorite spots was around my lower leg almost near the ankles. Fewer nerves are near the surface there. I don't think I did it because I wanted to feel pain; it was almost an escape though. When I did it, I couldn't focus on the mental problems I was having because I had bigger things to worry about. I was bleeding and my automatic response was to seek help and stop the bleeding. The mind can be funny that way. It can torment you to the point of wanting to kill yourself, yet at the first sign of physical pain, it stops. It demands you seek help for the physical issue. This cutting was a phase I went through, and it did not really help me feel better about myself. If anything the fact that I did this made me feel even worse about myself and feel like more of a pathetic loser.

Justin A. Mercer

CHAPTER 5
GOD, SUMMER CAMP, AND TALL LADDERS

The summer between sophomore and junior year was a defining summer for me. I went into it with high hopes. Sadly, those hopes would be dashed to pieces through a series of events that were simultaneously in and out of my control.

For starters, my girlfriend broke up with me. I never did get a reason why, but since she was beautiful and had a lot of attention from other guys coupled with my constant negative attitude must have made it a really easy choice for her. So she left. My first serious relationship was over in the blink of an eye through a text message at midnight: teenage love at its finest. If only it were that simple… I chose then of all times to fall apart. I sort of had a meltdown and couldn't handle myself. I didn't know what to do, so I ended up calling her and leaving a voicemail where I said some rather hurtful and regretful things. All the anxiety, sadness, and anger I had bottled up inside me, I unleashed in that voicemail. To this day I regret doing that. I can't even in good consciousness blame this explosion of emotion on depression, that would feel like a cop out and I do my best to not use this as a crutch. Still, had I not been depressed I would like to think I would have handled myself better.

A few days after the breakup and meltdown, I went to a camp that was usually one of my happier places. It was a Christian organization called REACH. I had been once the past summer and enjoyed it thoroughly. This group does some great work. Every summer they get an underpaid staff of college age kids to haul construction equipment across the country to shack up on the floors of high schools in the middle of nowhere America. All of this while organizing and running a camp of about 300-500 middle to high school aged kids that were here to help the local communities by rebuilding houses and such. If you are a Christian of middle school to high school age and you feel a desire to serve others, I highly suggest you look into it. I would also ask that you do not judge the program based on my experience.

This was the summer of 2010, and I was already coming into the week that was supposed to be dedicated to service and

God feeling worse than usual. Of course I fell into the moping crowd of other people who had just gotten broken up with recently. We were such a happy bunch to be around... looking back, the beginning of that week I remind myself of the Goth Kids from the TV show South Park, always talking about pain and suffering to the point of it being comedic to the outside observer.

Coming into this week, I had already begun to distance myself from church. Yet, I still had enough faith left to get through the nightly worships and enjoy them. I felt good from doing the service projects. As I stated earlier, I enjoy helping people. There is something about giving of myself to others that makes me feel good. Maybe it was another way of a cry for help, but to this day I don't think it was. Helping others makes me feel "right" and as a person that rarely ever gets to experience feeling "right" it felt even better.

Even during this week of rightness and good feelings, I could not keep my negativity and negative feelings down. I frequently found myself doing the most dangerous jobs I could find. Why? I think it was to distract myself from my mental torment, just as the cutting had been. You are forced to concentrate when 30 feet up in the air on a ladder that is dangerously close to power lines. Yes, I placed it there. The adult in charge of my work party tried to demand I get down. I wouldn't. I stayed up there until I was done painting the area that needed paint. I laughed in the face of danger. My self-preservation skills were good, but frequently I got myself, quite on purpose, into situations where I might need them.

I don't really want to spoil REACH for any reader who might potentially attend, because even though I am not religious, I do not want to rob you or demean you for your faith. So the short version of REACH's worship program is that it all builds to one big cathartic religious experience at the end of the week. I have left plenty to the imagination as not to spoil it for anyone, but I hope you readers understand the end result.

For a few hours there I felt good. I had confessed my sins to God. I told him I was tired of being sad and that I wanted help. I wanted it to be gone. Sadly, the feelings returned the next day, later that night even. I couldn't even finish a day without "being negative" as my mom called it at this stage in my life.

This is the point I truly started losing my religion. "That was me in the corner. That was me in the spot light"…I just wanted that line for the song reference. In actuality a better phrase would be: that was when I really started losing my faith. A song from the Episcopal Church's Maundy Thursday service came to mind on the long bus ride home. I wanted to feel as good as I did for those few hours all the time, and I didn't. I had slumped back into what I considered normal. Normal was negative. Normal was not happy. I do not know the name of the song, but I can clearly remember the baritone soloists haunting voice as all the candles in the church were extinguished and the lights are put out singing: "my God, my God, why have you forsaken me?"

That is the easiest way to sum up my feelings about religion at this time. I sort of still believed, but I also felt abandoned by God, and to top it off those feelings made me feel worse. I felt abandoned by God, so I was down about that, I was mad at myself for even considering that possibility so I made myself feel worse by hating myself, and then I felt bad about hating myself. This is a terrible cycle, you feel bad about feeling bad and then you feel bad about the fact that you felt bad, so you feel even worse. The cycle keeps repeating and you keep pulling yourself further and further down deeper into depression. Until I had someone put it into words for me, I did not know that I was doing this. It just sort of happened and I would be constantly on the downward slope into further negativity. This was a daily occurrence and it was my normal.

If this cycle describes you, the reader, in anyway, stop here, put the book down, and begin thinking about getting help. I know it can be hard to ask for help, especially about a mental condition. You may not feel you need help right now, I understand that. I didn't get help. I did not even think anything was wrong with me, I just assumed this was normal; this was how life is for everyone. Even if all you do is tell a friend or a loved one that "I am not happy," sometimes that may be enough to get a conversation started. Save yourself a lot of pain. It will be tough to say something initially, but it will be easier after that. Trust me; if you try and keep this to yourself it only gets worse.

Why did I not take my own advice you may be wondering? I was not yet "self-aware". I still believed that this was just how life was. Depression was just some alien thing that happened to people in novels like *One Flew Over the Cuckoo's Nest*. I never considered it a possibility as something that could happen to me. It was something that happened to other people, crazy people. At this point the symptoms of my mental illness were "not that bad"… Take that phrase with a grain of salt. My version of "incredibly bad" will be shown later in the book. At this time, I didn't hate life fully, but I was on the road towards that. I didn't like life. My symptoms were still bad, and an everyday fact of life, but the true "dark times" had yet to surface. Life was still not enjoyable, though it had no real reason not to be. All of the signs for depression were there. To be perfectly honest though, I did not even recognize them. This negativity was just normal for me. So again, if this describes you, you might be depressed. If it does, start fighting back now before it gets any harder. Depression, like most dreaded tests, is cumulative.

One main event in my life that ran through my 9th and 10th and 11th grade years was the absence of my dad. Due to the collapse of the economy in 2008 and especially the collapse of the auto industry, everything that my dad had built in his company vanished nearly overnight. After the collapse, my dad fought like hell to keep his company. He kept it going for about a year through his sheer willpower. Eventually though, he had to face the facts and close the doors to Mercer Industrial Sales.

This was obviously a massive blow to the family. My dad was jobless. He would hunt for almost a year to find a job. Quite frankly that year sucked. My mom cried a lot, and my dad had an almost hollow look in his eyes. He never gave up though. I admire him because he is my father, but I admire him even more for how he handled this whole terrible situation. Eventually in my 10th grade year my dad took a job in Atlanta, Georgia with Siemens. Siemens is one of those massive companies that does something in almost every industry. It was a good find for my dad at the moment, the only problem was that it was in Atlanta... about 150 miles away from home.

My dad absolutely refused to uproot our family and move to Atlanta. Instead he made the incredible sacrifice of commuting to Atlanta each week. During that time he lived in the guest bedroom of my grandparents' house. Not his parents, my mom's. He lived with his mother in law. While we have a great relationship with that part of my family, and they obviously love my dad, it is still hard to move into your parent in-laws house. Having talked to my dad recently, I know he feels partly responsible for my depression issues. It would not have changed anything if he was in Birmingham with me. I feel that I would have continued on the trajectory I was on with or without my dad living at home. He was doing what he had to do to keep our family from losing everything. I could never fault him for that, and if anything I love him more for it. I know that job was terrible and it killed him being away all the time. On the bright side of this I became much closer with my mom than I had been before.

The downside to all of this was that I was able to feel and see firsthand the economic impact of the recession on my family. Suddenly, I felt the financial burden of my education on my shoulders. Private school costs a ton of money and I realized what my parents were giving up to keep me in the school I was in. My mind managed to warp this and feel all the stress on myself, that the situation my family was in was my fault. Some blame Bush, some blame Obama, I blamed myself. To top it off, my grades were not even that great. That fact further added to my feelings of guilt, failure, and my overall stress. I realized this, and then became angry at myself for making it about me during a family crisis. Naturally all of this just fueled the depression.

CHAPTER 6
11TH GRADE- IT LOOKED EASIER IN THE MOVIES

For the longest time I had problems with girls. Early on in my high school career, I was the youngest guy in the class, a nerd, and looking back today without the veil of depression I know that I looked nothing like David Beckham. Couple all of those uncool factors together and I only was able to get face time with girls when they had history homework questions. It sucked, but many American teenagers, boys and girls, find themselves on the "not" side of the "hot or not" scale. I was not unique in that regard. Still though, us "nots" have to press on and try our best in the complex world of relationships.

By about the time I was a junior I was determined to take my interest in girls from "interest" to "actually doing something about it". Of course there were certain barriers to my perceived entry into the dating pool.

Depression can alter your view of yourself. I was obviously no supermodel, but in my eyes I was the Grinch or Quasimodo from the Hunchback of Notre Dame. My self-image was terrible. Not only was my perception of my physical self terrible, I also had a poor outlook on everything else I brought to the table. Being a self-professed nerd with the ability to quote Star Wars: A New Hope almost line for line is not a big selling point. The ability to give inane details about the Battle of Trafalgar or tell the story of the French Revolution was also not a selling point I wanted to make. That is all I thought I had to offer. Being two types of nerd in one. Yet, looking back I see I have done so many really cool things that other people still find cool. By 11th grade of high school I had been lucky enough to travel to eight different countries, white water raft through the Grand Canyon, be awarded the rank of Eagle Scout in the Boy Scouts of America, I was running cross country on the varsity squad and had been tapped to be the next team captain… I was just too blinded by depression which fed my negative self-image to see that I might have been cool.

Obviously thinking you bring nothing to the table and thinking you look like an Orc from Lord of the Rings sort of kills your self-confidence. As cliché as it sounds, confidence is apparently important when you're trying to date as I would find out time and time again.

My biggest issue is my failure to act. Since I thought I was useless and was selling something that no female in her right mind would want, I obviously did not have the confidence to ask many of the girls that I liked out. When I did manage to ask one out, I was usually stammered and stuttered my way through the question and was rejected. The most common scenario though was that I would be to terrified of being a "failure" and wouldn't think myself worthy so I wouldn't ask the "her" of the moment out.

So it came to pass that junior year my guy friends gave me the nickname "Captain Friendzone". I know there is a massive debate on the internet of whether there is actually a friendzone, and that just because a guy is nice doesn't mean he deserves to get with a girl. Trust me, I get that. No, I didn't feel entitled to a relationship because I try and be kind to everyone, and I take most of the blame for getting myself to the friendzone. I was not trying to get stamps on my "Nice Guy Card" with the goal of reaching the magic number to convince a girl to go out with me. I was just so negative going into anything that I couldn't possibly make my feelings for any girl known. If I thought of myself in such a negative light, how could any rational girl possibly like me? There were more than a few times when I would try and start the "Look, I like you, wanna date?" conversation and never got further into my well scripted speech than saying hi. I didn't believe I would succeed anyway so it became a self-fulfilling prophecy. "I am ugly inside and out. She is beautiful. She would not want to be with me anyway. Why am I like this. I hate myself."

At least my ultra- negative predictions about this situation that somehow started with me talking to a girl, and then ended in a Russian nuclear strike never came to pass. Yes, there were times that I was that negative about this. Humor helped me deal with my failure.

I spent most of my highs school dating career shooting myself repeatedly in the foot with a cannon... Since I was so down on myself and pessimistic about my chances, it was rare that I actually asked a girl out. Even if the girl of the moment liked me beforehand, my inaction led her to believe I did not like her at all, makes total sense. Dating, even the entirety of high school social life, looked much easier in the movies.

The cycle continued its downward spiral from there. Since I apparently wasn't interested, the girl I liked would end up with someone else. Usually a good friend or someone I hated. I honestly can't tell you which is worse…I would become angry at myself for my inaction and angry in general. I was angry at myself because I was me. "Why should he get her and not me? There must be something wrong with me" would be my thought process. I would hate myself for being a coward and not asking her out or telling her how I felt. I would then be more depressed than usual because of all that was going on in my mind. Then the cycle would start over. Every time I would replay the events in my mind the cycle kept pulling me further and further down. The blackness would creep into every corner of my soul and bring me to new lows. Master Yoda says it best: "Fear leads to Anger, Anger leads to Hate, and Hate leads to Suffering."

The thing with depression is that it pretty much is one long sum of these things I have been referring to as "cycles". Your mind does not play fair; it can call up any of your past mistakes at will and add those to the ongoing cycle. In the end it isn't just one of these "cycles" pulling you down, it can be tens, hundreds, thousands. It can be so many that they become a deluge and it isn't possible for you to think of all of them at once, they just keep flicking through your mind, each one dragging you further and further down, and no matter what you cannot escape. You are trapped being tortured by this deluge of negativity in the most secure prison in the world: your mind. I imagine this is what waterboarding feels like.

These relationship or relationship failure cycles would add up over time. With each failure the ensuing deluge of thoughts would get worse and worse. That was true with everything that brought me down, all my failures, all my shortcomings. The longer I was depressed, the worse off it became.

This is why I advise that if you feel any sort of depression, even if it is only "minor", to find a way to help yourself now. Reader, I probably do not know you, and I may never will, I do know that you do not deserve to feel that way. Every human on this planet deserves to feel free in their own mind, to have the ability to experience happiness. Reader, if you are currently feeling how I described myself feeling in the previous long paragraph, please do what I didn't, and find a way out now. I promise you it does not get any easier the longer you wait, it only gets harder. Yes, it can get worse. Why suffer? Start fighting back now.

Again, I did not take my own advice. How could I? I did not even stop to consider that there might be something else going on that made me "so negative all the time." I would consider my junior year of high school a major tipping point. This is when my mental state began getting worse at what felt like a geometric rate. The days became longer and longer, and each one was harder and harder. On top of the numerous relationship failures I experienced, I also experienced the dissolution of my friend group. High school drama at its finest. Looking back, it might have made a great sitcom TV show... I ended up caught in the middle of this split and at times felt like each side was warring over me for my friendship. Either way it was a lot of high school drama, and I somehow convinced myself that a situation entirely out of my control was my fault, and that I was a failure because I could not repair everyone's friendships. This began another series of "cycles" to add to the increasing deluge of them going on in my mind. Did I mention that about 80% of my friends were graduating at the end of the year? Yes, most of these people were seniors. I feared that I would be incredibly lonely my senior year. I was angry at my perceived inability to make other friends, especially within my grade. I hated myself for being afraid that I would be lonely because I should have confidence in myself. Naturally all of these thoughts added to the torture in my mind and I suffered for it. See the pattern yet? Event, unwanted and unwarranted negative thoughts that I assumed were truth, suffering, depression. Wash, rinse, and repeat.

CHAPTER 7
HEATED DEBATES

The summer between junior and senior year was a continuation of all the drama of the school year. I was caught in the middle of many rapidly dissolving friendships, I was worried about my own very uncertain future as a senior, oh and "Captain Friendzone" did nothing to help himself lose that nickname. One other thing I experienced in that summer was the almost complete loss of religion as something of any importance in my life. This wasn't a conscious choice of mine. As I had explained I had been losing faith for a long time. Having a negative outlook on life makes it hard to believe in an all loving God. This summer I would go to REACH for the last time. I'll admit to not wanting to go. I had sort of outgrown REACH in my mind, both age wise, and religious wise. I knew that I wasn't going to enjoy the religious factor so that I would have a boring week. I did still like helping people though, so I figured I could at least do some good, and that maybe a week away would do some good for me. My dad even decided to be an adult chaperone on the trip this time. That in itself was an interesting experience having him there. Since he had been away working in Atlanta for most of my high school years, it should have been a good week for us to reconnect.

I consider myself a fair person to deal with. At this time I certainly had a negative outlook on life and it tainted conversations and relationships, but if you wanted to engage me in a philosophical debate over an issue I would be happy to oblige. I have always loved the battle of wits that is a debate. I also just enjoy hearing people's opinions and views on the world. It helps me build my own worldview.

A little more backstory here, I promise this is going somewhere. I have long held the belief that "I don't care about your sexuality." If you are gay, great. I am not, please respect that and I'll respect you. I may not be entirely comfortable with homosexuality, but it is just a part of our world. As far as I am concerned everyone is just people and as long as your actions do not negatively affect me or others, then I am ok with it. Do I have to be comfortable with everything?

No, but I will still stand up for your right to be your own person. I also believe in your right to disagree with me and with everyone. Different opinions and the right to have those different opinions are what makes this country great. M'urica. My one rule: don't be an asshole.

At REACH my propensity for getting into philosophical debates would end up getting me "in trouble." The lady that was the adult chaperone of my work crew was... ultra-religious and ultra-conservative. There is nothing inherently wrong with that. What is wrong is attempting to force your beliefs on other people, that goes for both sides of the aisle. Believe what you will, but please do not attempt to ram your beliefs down my throat.

Of course, that is exactly what happened. This lady began spouting off hate and vile towards gay people to our group (some of these kids were 13) and I decided to give the other side of the argument to be truly fair and balanced in an attempt to let them form their own opinions. This argument continued over the course of the week. I admitted to the group that I was not very religious and that if I was that I would not take the bible literally. I poked the figurative bear... I ended up having to defend my position as a "fag lover" and deal with the group leader by her trying to "save me from the devil" all week. Need I remind you this was at a camp that I paid for to go to a town in rural, poor Ohio that I will probably never go to again to help someone I will never meet again. Selfless service... I have actually read the bible and I feel like Jesus would be happy that I was out there doing exactly what he was trying to do. His fan club though did not think I was doing right. Being berated all week and being told I am a terrible person and should suffer for it because of my beliefs kind of sucks. As a depressed person who was used to having this camp be a respite from the depression it was terrible. I did not need to hear this. I did not need every day to be a fight against a crusade of hatred. Bigotry won't help me change my opinion. At the end of the week the lady that was my work team's chaperone had turned the team against me because I was "not a good influence and needed to be saved by the power of Christ." Over the course of my life I have had many adults say that I am a "great young man" and that "more kids should be like me," all of those compliments were unasked for.

Naturally the only things that stuck in my mind were the negative.

On the last day of working on our project during our lunch break which had become "religiously abuse Justin time" she told me in front of the whole group that if I did not change my ways I would burn in hell for eternity. I told her that I was not going to be intimidated into changing my beliefs. She flat out told me that I was going to Hell and that she was sorry and would "pray for my eternal soul." Keep in mind that I was still only sixteen.

Since I am not really religious, it did not hurt on that level, but it still stung. I had been giving of myself freely that week. I had been trying to live a good life. If someone told me that I was going to hell today I would laugh and probably bust out into a certain AC/DC song. Back then, it hurt: this group of people I have never met before think I am the scum of the earth after knowing me for a week. They thought I was so bad that they wanted me to burn in a fiery pit and inhale sulfur for all eternity. This was after only having met me a week ago. I must be a bad person. Why am I a bad person? It must just be who I am. I guess I don't deserve happiness then. I am not happy. I do not want to come back here. Nothing stays happy forever. Even the good times get tainted. No, I am the one who taints the good times. I am the problem.

As an aside to everyone out there, damning people to hell is not an effective way to get them to believe what you want. Especially when you keep throwing around the phrases "god of love" and "god of mercy, "prince of peace" is an especially funny one. The sales pitch I was given to this god of love sounded more like I was being read an execution statement. I am a different case because I was depressed anyway, but please consider what you are going to say before you say it. You don't know what damning someone to hell will do to them. Even if you think they or I are going to hell, you don't have to tell me. By attempting to "save" me, I was hurt more. Rethink how you want to "save" people. Maybe sticking with a true message of love instead of spouting hatred would help your case. That goes for all religions, not just Christianity. I was at a time in my life when I could have used some extra love; instead I was greeted with hellfire and damnation. I did that to myself enough already.

Back at the school where the campers were staying, my dad and the youth pastor from my hometown church noticed my extraordinarily downcast mood. They found the lady and reprimanded her and asked her to apologize to me saying what she did was inappropriate. She did not relent and refused to apologize even going as far as telling my father that he raised a heathen who would burn in hell. She walked away leaving my father and the youth pastor, who both sincerely believe in a loving god, flabbergasted. They both sat with and tried to console me that night. Unfortunately it was too late for me. In my mind god had already ceased to exist. In trying to "win my soul for god" that lady had killed god for me.

That experience haunts me still. That lady, in her misguided efforts to save my soul had not only crushed the small amount of faith I might have had for her god, but she had taken away a place and time that was supposed to be happy for me. In a life clouded by unchecked depression true happiness is rare. Taking away a time and place that was supposed to let me reconnect with my father, reconnect with my faith, and be happy giving myself to others was a huge blow to me. I thought senior year was going to be a rough ride.

CHAPTER 8
SENIORS 2012

One August morning in 2011, I woke up and I was cool. It was a long process to get here, but here I was. I was that cool senior that almost everyone in the lower grades thought was awesome. It all started at the end of my junior year. Since I went to a private school we did things a little differently. For one, we were a boarding and day school. Since I lived about seven miles from school there was no reason for me to live on campus, plus it added a lot of money to the already considerable cost of tuition.

Well thankfully for me I had managed to pull my grades up and actually get good enough grades to get a scholarship to live on campus for my senior year. In return for my free room and board, I would be a student leader in the dorms. Someone that people looked up to. Also at the end of junior year I entered my name into the school elections. I had tried my hand a few times previously for the easy positions and had not been elected. This time I was running for the most "popular" position: Commissioner of Service. The "COS" is a position at my school that was in charge of running the Student Store. Usually there are two of them since it is such a big job.

Essentially I sold candy, coke, and chips to those that wanted them in between classes and on breaks. Since it was a position that dealt with the majority of the school all the time, and this was a high school election naturally it was a popularity contest. Sadly no, this is not a story of the quiet nerd and his friend coming into his own and beating out the traditional ringleaders of the popular kid crowd for a vaunted position. This is a story of political ruthlessness almost worthy of "House of Cards" or "Game of Thrones".

My running mate and I were at the mandatory meeting for candidates on time as we were supposed to be. Ten minutes late into the meeting the two popular kids walk in with their petition and platform to run. Those were due at the start of the meeting and the deadline was strict. The faculty member running the meeting was still willing to accept their petition though. Believing that if they were allowed to run; my ticket would lose, I shouted down the petition on the grounds that they were late. Well the rules stated in black and white that I was right. My running mate and I waltzed into the job unopposed. Normally an act like this would help fuel my depression because I would be angry at myself because I didn't "fight fair" or keep to my "honor" or something like that. Usually those things legitimately worry me, if I wasn't depressed they would. I believe in honor and fairness, but in this case... these two guys were not the main perpetrators of my 8th and 9th grade torture, but they did help play a part whether they know it or not. I guess since they were part of the "popular" crowd they also assumed it was okay to be condescending and an ass to everyone "below" them all the time. Well it was time for a little revenge of the nerds, so I lost no sleep over my ruthless high school politicking.

So here I was a senior, a dorm leader, Captain of the cross country team, and in a position of power in charge of the student store, and of course the promised land of college lying just beyond the horizon. What happened? I got...cool? I had it made. For all my worrying at the end of junior year and throughout the summer this was a very refreshing surprise. How could this dream year possibly get messed up?

I would be lying if I said this was not one of the best, if not the best year of my life. Looking back though, it could have been better, so much better. While many great things happened, there were also some down points, but that is life and these things happen. The difference with me and a person not afflicted with depression is how they take it. On the surface, my life was amazing, even with most of the setbacks, I felt like I owned the school. The halls that I used to slink around and try and hide away I now roamed as if I were a demi-god. No doubt my senior year was amazing. Junior year had been a mess caught in a downward spiral. Yet here was senior year going much better than I expected. There were times I felt truly happy this year. Still though, even the brightest happiness was tainted with the darkness of depression. It was still there, and this year would ultimately set me up for some of the darkest days of my life.

Now to dive into the ups and downs of the rollercoaster that was my senior year. I started the year off as if I had just ascended to the throne of the Roman Empire. Hail Caesar. For the first time when people said I was "awesome" or "cool" I actually let myself believe them a little. I strutted around; I could hold a conversation with anyone I wanted too in almost any social circle. It amazed me how I wanted nothing more than to leave this school almost three years ago, and here I was now as arguably one of the most influential seniors. Yes, I am laying it on a bit thick here, and I am definitely talking myself up, but the transformation in my own eyes was amazing. Then things began to unravel.

The first thing to happen would be my running mate/partner in charge of the student store would be one of the first school officers to be asked/forced to step down. Coincidentally he was also one of my four roommates that year.

One night about midway through the fall semester, my roommates decided to have a party to celebrate one of their 18th birthdays. They decided to have it in our dorm room suite. We were in a high school dorm; parties of this nature were of course a major rule violation. I had never been much of a partier, and had only tried my first liquor a few weeks earlier in the same suite. For whatever reason I had the good sense or luck not to partake that night, I quietly went to bed. I couldn't really sleep because the geniuses were being incredibly loud. Apparently they forgot that a faculty member had their house on the other side of the wall from us... Morning came; I woke up, walked past a person passed out on our suite common room couch, rolled my eyes and went to class. I didn't care if they had a party. I've always been cool with partiers and smokers, I almost had to be. Since they were the majority of my school population I almost didn't have a choice. Yes I was a bit of a goody two shoes that didn't smoke or didn't drink, but for once I really am glad I was.

I found out later that day that my roommates had been caught, not in the act, but after the fact. They decided to dispose of the multitude of glass bottles and red solo cups in the dorm dumpster using a clear trash bag. The same dumpster used by the faculty that live next to the dorm to oversee it. That would not have been a problem, it's not like the school could trace any of the alcohol remnants back to our dorm room. You would need a name for that to even begin to know where to start looking...

Well the school had a name, how? My roommates had

thrown the party stuff out with their normal trash. One of the guys had left his birthday card in the trash. The school had a name. My roommates were screwed, and for a few hours there I thought I would be too. Thankfully these guys were all good friends and I still try and keep in contact with them. While their stories to the faculty varied, they all agreed on one thing, I was not involved.

So about this time, I bet you are wondering how this story could make my life worse. I had no part in this fiasco and wasn't punished for it. Well, not directly anyway. All of my roommates held some sort of leadership position, whether it was as Proctor (the top student leader in the dorm) or as my partner as Commissioners of Service in running the student store. The school stripped them of their positions, since they broke one of the major rules it was really a fair punishment. They also got suspended. Don't worry though, they all came back and made it to college just fine. I'm pretty sure two of them have full rides. So the school needed someone to take over those positions, I was promoted to Proctor, told that I would be running the student store myself from now on, and pretty much told good luck with that.

But that all benefitted me right? My politicking and Machiavellian tactics had gotten me more power which is exactly what I was talking about enjoying earlier, right? Hail Caesar? Truth be told, no it wasn't fun. I was doing a two man job running the student store by myself, I had Proctor duties now, and I still had to make time to be captain of the cross country team, not to mention school and attempting to secure scholarships for and get into college. I was constantly overwhelmed and under serious pressure.

There is only so much one person can do without help, and I had reached my limit. I told my science teacher/cross country coach since 9th grade, that I was going to be five minutes late to practice every day because I had to shut down the student store. She was perfectly okay with this. Unfortunately she had some medical issues going on with her foot (a key part of running and walking) and she had been an absentee coach for most of the season. I had been in charge of running the team practices myself and doing what she told me. It was just one more responsibility, but I was okay with it. Eventually she decided it was in the best interest of the team and she resigned so the school could find a new coach. A perfectly normal and respectable decision, I could not dream of faulting her for it though I wish she had stayed as coach. This coaching regime change came at an incredible cost to me though. This 'amazing' year was slowly starting to unravel.

The new coach started practice earlier than I did, so I told him I would be late because of my responsibilities with the student store. He immediately questioned my commitment to the team. I earned no favors with the fact that I was not actually the strongest runner. I believe my best 5k time was 21 minutes and change. I nearly died after running that pace , but it was a respectable average time. I usually averaged 23-26 minutes. I looked bad as a runner and a captain, especially since I had been doing this since 9th grade. I am just not the best distance runner.

This fact quickly got under the new coach's skin. He expected me to be the fastest on the team because I was captain. There were some kids on the team that simply lived to run though. I will never complete a 5k in less than 20 minutes, much less fewer than 18. These kids did. They are great runners, the only thing is: they were freshman, sophomores and juniors. Some of them had only started running on the team that year. I was the only senior on the team. I had worked and waited since my freshman year for the captaincy. There aren't even any perks with being captain, it is just a title and you are recognized as team leader. In fact it is more responsibility and no perks. The captain did not even get an identifying mark on their jersey. So one of my team mates had me put a duct tape "C" on it for fun. While it had no advantages, being captain was still a goal that I had worked hard to achieve, and it was about to be taken away from me.

I got an email towards the end of cross country season, so late October, to come and talk to my science teacher/ former cross country coach. For a time reference, the entire party debacle and my subsequent increase in responsibility happened in early September. I walked in there, obviously nervous. I never get called into teacher's offices. Well I sort of knew what to expect going in there. I had missed practice a few times that week because I was doing things for the student store. I believe I was trying to implement an actual inventory system so that I knew what I had… Plus, it was a very small school. I sort of heard about it on my walk to the office. Nearly in tears, my teacher told me that I was being removed from the captaincy in the nicest way she possibly could. It wasn't her fault, and it wasn't her choice. I think the new coach was an asshole for making her deliver the message instead of giving it to me in person. I had known this teacher since 5th grade and had been friends and going to school with her son since that time. This was hard for her; she had pretty much seen me grow up. I was told that I shouldn't even bother going to practice anymore, but that they would let me run in the final races if I wanted too. Later that afternoon I walked into her office again and turned in my jersey. It still had the duct taped "C" on it over my heart that one of my teammates insisted I put there . I walked out almost in tears. I think she was sad about it too.

I was afraid that I had been a failure, that surely there must have been something I could have done to keep this from happening. I was angry at myself for having not been able to balance all of my responsibilities. I was angry at the new coach and the old one for destroying years of my hard work. I hated myself for the loss of my position and pretty much being kicked out of something I loved. It became a cycle that I would repeat over and over in my head.

I was afraid about my performance running the student store, never mind the fact that it was the most successful it had been in years. I felt under the microscope about everything I did these days because I was not caught as part of the earlier drinking debacle. The administration was simply waiting for me to screw up. They thought I was a partier and drug user because of who my friends were. I was not a party goer in high school. It was an unfair assumption. Yet I always received scathing glances from the administration and think some of them never believed that I was telling them the truth when I spoke to them. I was fed up and angry at the two person job of running the store that I was doing singlehandedly without a single thanks or nod of appreciation. I hated the fact that this job had cost me my cross country position. This became a cycle that I would repeat over and over in my head.

Ironically the next semester's COSs would have some problems and "lose" all of the money I had made for the store. I was told by the administration that I was going to help run the store because clearly they needed my help. Irony at its finest.

CHAPTER 9
HUNTING FOR COLLEGE

I went to a high school that usually sends a good number of people to Ivy League schools and other 'good' colleges. The three I applied to were: Colorado State, Auburn University, and Appalachian State, a list lacking in prestigious universities. My first choice was Colorado State. A few of my friends had gone there including a girl that Captain Friendzone had been into for a long time. So yes, I was doing a dumb thing and trying to follow a girl to college. A girl that I was not in, nor have I ever had a relationship with, I did not even declare my like for this girl. Looking back, I am kind of glad events played out the way they did. I am glad that coming events would take place in state and not way off in Colorado. I had a lot to get through before I would realize that though.

The economic crash drained my family's college fund for important things like school, mortgage payments, gas, and food. Unless I wanted to plunge myself or my parents into crippling debt, it was absolutely imperative that I get a scholarship. I applied for tons of them. I knew I couldn't afford Colorado State, or almost any college without them. So it came to pass towards the end of the first semester of my senior year I was accepted into all three schools I had applied for, now to wait on scholarships.

The main scholarship I was banking on was a four year full ride Army ROTC scholarship. Am I a soldier type? Not really. Okay not at all. Did I believe I could do it for the four years required of me? Yes. The Army gives these scholarships to specific schools and you are allowed to make a choice between those schools that they select. I had made it through the interviews, the psychological profile (ironic), the essays, and the physical fitness tests. On the day the results were posted I frantically checked my computer.

"Congratulations Justin Mercer, You have been extended an offer of a 3-year scholarship at these colleges and universities: Auburn University." None of it is what I wanted to hear. I never thought my heart could sink at the fact that I had won a great honor. I felt like I had lost. I wasn't going to Colorado now. I could not afford it. I was going to Auburn. The one school that I did not want to go to, but I applied to it as my backup. I called my mom; she was ecstatic at first but then after hearing the straining in my voice, she realized the implications of what I had said. So just like that a dream evaporated. The dream of living out in the beautiful state of Colorado, snowboarding on weekends, hiking in the mountains, and of course being out there with friends. All of my delusions of grandeur were gone.

I wasn't good enough to get the full scholarship to where I wanted to go therefore I must not be good enough for anything. I fear for my future as it is now more uncertain than ever. I am angry at myself for not being better. I am angry at myself for believing I could do this. I hate myself for being who I am. I hate how I could not run faster, or say the right thing in the interview. I let myself down. I hate myself. I hate myself…

On "college day", a day towards the end of second semester when the seniors all wear shirts of the college that they will be going to, I wore an Auburn shirt. I had resigned myself to the "War Eagle" fate, and I had also accepted the Army ROTC scholarship. Three years paid for was better than no years paid for. It didn't matter if they would own me for a few years following college, I could do this. I am strong and self-confident. I am going to be the best damn soldier the US Army has ever seen.

Before I could go off and be a hero of the college campus, I would have to graduate high school. Oddly enough there was a threat that it wouldn't happen. As a senior class "we" screwed up bad. It is tradition for the senior class to have a prank on campus and then most leave and go to a party or something. My friends and I having already experienced one pitfall with drinking during the year were probably just going to chill afterwards because we could. Well the idea is to do the prank and then have the party off campus. Naturally our class barely did the prank and held the party on campus… It ended rather suddenly when a girl wrecked her car on a decorative boulder that was on a side walk and nowhere near the road. I saw it the next day. A little foreign car managed to drag this two ton boulder a good 25 feet. It ripped out the transmission, front axle, gas tank, and finally lodged underneath the rear axle. Since this was a rear wheel drive the momentum the car must have had… Anyway, the call went out that this girl had wrecked a car and cops were coming. There were tons of alcohol and drugs on campus that night. So my friends and I fled to the only safe haven nearby: Waffle House.

The next day our entire class was bent over the proverbial table by the administration. They were almost indiscriminate with their hatred towards us. If you were on campus at all that night you were just as at fault. I would like to point out that the entire school and administration knew we were on campus. Most of them live on campus themselves and could easily hear the ruckus going on. That did not matter though. We were a disgrace to the school. The traditional "Toast to the Teachers" ceremony where we thank the teachers that we have grown close to over the years was canceled because they did not want to hear our "empty and hollow words." They nearly canceled our last dance and the closest thing we have to prom: Senior Banquet. I was going to be pissed if they did because a girl had actually asked me if I wanted to go with her. I didn't care if it was just as friends, I was just happy that finally I had a date to a damn dance, even if it was my last one ever. Seriously, this was the first time I took a girl to a dance, and it came in the dying days of senior year.

The administration and teachers laid into us for about an hour while we sat there silent. It truly hurt to have these figures that I looked up to and admired greatly indiscriminately hurling this hatred at us. I admired them so much, that I want to be a teacher just like them. I know as a class "we" messed up. Still the fact that they were about as discriminate as an atom bomb hurt those of us who were not truly at fault. Ironically for me, this lambasting did not contribute much to my overall depression, but everyone was in a dour mood at this point. They had just threatened to cancel graduation. My only guess of why this didn't affect me that much was because I truly knew I was not to blame.

On that interesting note my senior year was wrapped up. I had the most beautiful date at Senior Banquet. Since we were only going as friends and since one of my best bros and his date were only going as friends, and we both knew we had zero chance in hell of getting lucky… I mean, I had the most beautiful date at the dance. I went to the ball with a girl that could easily play Cinderella if they ever made a live action movie. I know for self-confidence purposes I shouldn't consider girls "out of my league," but she was definitely out of my league. I would love to make an analogy of this in terms of soccer, but sadly most people in America are not massive soccer fans. So for this sports analogy, it would be a game of football: Appalachian State vs. the New England Patriots. That is how far out of my league this girl was. She was Cinderella at the ball and I did my best to play the part of Prince Charming. For someone as terrible at women as I am, having a girl go to a dance with me was a major victory… After the dance my friend and I dropped our dates off at various parties and went to see a movie, "The Dictator", in theatres. Why? Because neither of us had any hope of getting any, so what better way to live out a sad reality than by watching a hilarious movie?

The summer between senior year and college, I worked. That is pretty much all I did. I was still pervasively unhappy and lacked self-confidence, but I was not in deep depression all the time. While I consider this a good chapter of my life, I know it could have been better. I could have had the courage to ask a girl out. I could have tried harder and not let myself feel overwhelmed and caught up in depressive cycles because of it. I knew this at the time too. I was going to try and continue the awesomeness that had been my senior year in college. I had seen enough college movies to know that it was going to be cool. Even though it wasn't my first choice, I still was excited for this new chapter in my life. It was time to turn the page. Hello Freshman Cadet History major Mercer.

CHAPTER 10
COLLEGE FRESHMAN: THE 9TH CIRCLE OF HELL

In Dante's Inferno, the 9th level of hell is cold, dark; at the center of it the 4th layer of the circle is Satan himself with three others. All of them betrayers: Judas Iscariot, Brutus, and Cassius. It is arguably the worst level of hell. It is the furthest from the stars and the heavens, and even the furthest from God. There is no good in the world here. Satan himself is crying as are the three men he holds in his clutches as he gnaws away at them and their very souls forever and for eternity. It is black and cold. Ice is everywhere, Satan and the other betrayers are frozen in a massive hellish lake called Cocytus. Satan beats his massive wings as if trying to escape, but it is in vain. All the wings do is kick up an icy wind. Dante and Virgil do not linger here long. They escape by climbing through a small hole in the ice and leaving through the bottom of hell on towards brighter things. I… I lingered in this circle of my own personal hell for a very long time.

I started out my first year of college as an oblivious but optimistic freshman. Not entirely as naïve as I was when starting high school, just a little more confident. Surely the future was bright. I had passed through the storm that was high school. College was finally here, and I wanted to succeed, in school, in the Army, with friends, and with girls. I moved into Knapp Hall in the Hill Residence Halls on Auburn University for the start of my freshman year. I did not know my roommate coming into this, we had chatted on Facebook once. He seemed ok.

So we moved in, and immediately did not get along. He was a good little frat guy wannabe. He was arrogant, pretentious, and a person who couldn't handle his sudden freedom, oh and a massive douchebag. Basically a stereotype for frat dudes. Since this time I have met some great and genuine people that have been involved in fraternities, but this guy…he just played the stereotype so well.

I didn't know this guy coming into this; I wanted to give him a chance. We knew we did not get along from the get go. Inside of three weeks we had even agreed to change roommates. He would move in with one of his frat wannabe buddies, and I would take the frat wannabe buddy's Navy ROTC roommate. Since I was Army ROTC it would work out. We both had PT the same mornings and kept roughly the same schedules. I was three days away from this move.

One Wednesday night my roommate came back more drunk than I had ever seen anyone. He kept screaming "I got a bid! I got a bid from Sigma Nu!! (Or was it Pi... Or Chi?) Sigma something. Anyway, the actual fraternity does not matter, I know now that he is not representative of the entire Greek life system. When he came back into the room, this guy was practically dead. He was throwing up because he can't hold his liquor. So in the spirit of doing something good, I got him a trash can, gave him one of my Gatorades and some of my crackers in an attempt to sober him up and make him not totally hate himself in the morning. He passed out hard. I went to sleep; I had class early in the morning.

I woke up around four AM to this guy standing at the side of my bed taking a piss on me, my backpack, and schoolbooks that were around my bed. I mean literally. He was literally pissing on me, as in urinating. I did what any sane person would do. I reflexively punched him to get him to stop. I also aimed a nice right hook at his desk lamp for good measure, yes it was overkill, but it was the lamp or his face and I'll be honest: I was madder than hell. His face would not have been pretty by the end of it. We started shouting at each other. That went on for about an hour. He refused to acknowledge what had just happened. He was still drunk. Eventually I got fed up and called the RA. The RA gets to the door and before I can say anything my roommate says: "He assaulted me and then threatened to kill me." Now I am sure that I said that. I was madder than hell and I wanted to kill him. In the middle of screaming insults at each other I am pretty damn sure I said something like "Shut the *I want to try and keep this book PG-13* up or I swear to god I will kill you." No, I was not serious in my threat. Yes, I hit him. This was the first physical fight I had ever been in, the fact that I was arguably successful in the physical part and that I knocked him back gives me laughs even today. The RA finally let me speak. I told him the story from the sober person's perspective. I admitted my "wrong" actions thinking that I would be let off the hook because I woke up to an underage drunk guy pissing on me and my couple hundred dollar textbooks. The RA was close to resolving the situation and was going to separate us for the rest of the night and let us move out tomorrow. Then my roommate decided that no, I should get in trouble now. He threatened to call a lawyer and swore that he was going to get me thrown out of Army ROTC and Auburn, if not go to jail. I panicked. My family did not have the money to face a lawsuit or a criminal trial. I started to wonder if I would have to defend myself in court or get a public defender. So I did what a lot seventeen year old's in serious trouble do...I called my dad.

No father wants to answer the phone at 5:30 in the morning with his son starting the conversation buy saying "Dad, do we have a lawyer?" My dad got to Auburn by 7:30 AM. When he showed up I had hustled over to the ROTC building and was talking to my commanding officer, a 1st Lieutenant, and trying to clear this with him, just letting him know what was happening. My Master Sergeant overheard the conversation from his office next door. He stuck his head in and said, "Should've just beaten the shit outta the guy. Then we wouldn't have had this problem. It's what I would have done," before disappearing down the hallway. That was the one laugh I would have that day.

After my dad arrived I was taken in front of the Director of Housing. She informed me that since I made a violent threat my case was being taken personally by the Dean of Students. This is a school of 25,000. Speaking to the Dean of Students is one step below the President. I was terrified. I felt like the victim here, and yet I was being crucified. I do not know what my now former roommate did that day. I think he hung out with his friends... That was one thing I did not have the luxury of having. At this point I had zero friends in Auburn. I had no one in a hundred miles on my side until my dad showed up.

The Dean of Students was actually very nice. She actually laughed when I told her the story and almost repeated word for word what the Master Sergeant had said. I did not find this as funny as she did. The entire day I was probably close to having an aneurism I was so stressed out. In the end, I was placed on housing probation, which meant that if I acted out again I would be kicked out of housing for sure and the University would be able to take further action at their discretion. I also had to write an essay saying how I was "wrong" and how I could have handled the situation better. I laced it with ample amounts of sarcasm and cynicism. The solution to keep me from being violent with a new roommate was to give me a room to myself in a different dorm. By the end of the day I had moved into Sassnett Hall room 420. I was so lost in my own mind that I did not even notice the fact that I had a humorous room number. My sense of humor was one of the first things to go. My future was dimming fast.

I enjoyed having a room to myself for about a week, if that. My depression that had flat lined during my senior had been slowly building up steam again in the first few weeks of college. Whereas I had experienced a deluge of negative thoughts before, now the dam broke. It was an unceasing torrent from the moment I woke up to the moment I went to sleep. Being completely isolated in a room did not help.

I hated ROTC. I hated my classes, I hated school, I hated Auburn, I hated everything. I hated myself. I hated being alive. I had no friends; I had acquaintances and people that I kind of knew. Some of them realized I was vulnerable. Some of my fellow cadets realized I was easy to make fun of. They launched a craigslist campaign as a prank against me. My name and phone number were attached to an ad that I was giving away a free monkey. Many hundreds of idiots called me that night. I got no sleep, but I rarely slept now anyway though I was always tired. I couldn't sleep. I could not shut off my mind. It was constantly barraging me with unasked for negative thoughts. I couldn't find the peace to fall asleep.

I admire all servicemen, yet I can't do it. I failed. I wanted to quit. I could not handle being told I was shit all the time. My platoon really was, and I was one of the worst. I could not handle it. Even when I did something right, someone else would screw up and we would be punished. The experience is supposed to bond us, but it just made us cadets hate each other. It might not have been as bad as I thought. I just saw it this way and felt it this way. To me, my existence was hell. I had the option to quit at the end of my first semester. I did not. I did not want to allow myself to be a failure.

Every day was a struggle to get out of bed. Not an "I'm still sleepy" struggle, I just had no willpower to move, I did not want to give in to the fact that I had to live for another day. If I could have stayed asleep I would have been fine. It took so long for me to fall asleep anyway that sleep was almost pointless. My mind would race night and day, a constant flood of these oppressive "cycles" that kept repeating and getting more and more vivid. More of these were added to my mind's repertoire of torture each day. Every little thing made my life worse. For example: I made awkward eye contact with a cute girl, suddenly I remember all of my failings with girls all at once. I am a failure. I hate the fact that I am bad at talking to girls. I hate myself. I loathe myself. I wish I was anyone but me. I hate that I can't escape this constant negative mental oppression. I hate myself because I am the only one to blame for this. I hate that I can't control my mind. I hate myself. I hate life. I don't want to live anymore.

In the time it took you to read that paragraph that one cycle or thought process would have completed and started over. It would join other cycles and thought processes and form a constant barrage of "I hate myself. I want to escape. I can't escape. If I were dead, I could escape." That was my daily torture, and each day added its own small problems to the already massive and constant stream of these thought processes going on in my head. It never stopped. It only stopped when I was asleep, and even then most nights I had fitful sleep anyway.

I remember tripping over a loose brick on the Haley Concourse one day. If you are an Auburn student, I would imagine you have tripped over a brick on the concourse too. I was unnaturally embarrassed. This one small mistake was like a dagger to the heart. Not necessarily the mundane action of tripping over a brick, but the avalanche of depressive thoughts it released. Tripping over a loose brick is probably one of the most normal human things anyone can do, and yet even that caused me to be dragged deeper into depression: tripping over a brick, a stupid brick.

I could not function. When I wasn't in class or doing something with ROTC I was in my room, alone, isolated. At least here in solitude it was hard for me to add things to the repeating depressive thoughts of my mind, or so I believed. In actuality it presented me with a whole new set of problems to add to my depression. I was lonely. I may have gone to a school of 25,000 but for all it mattered to me I could have been on a deserted island. I had no friends here. I don't think I allowed myself to have friends here after the very defining encounter with my roommate earlier on; I just sort of gave up. I clearly did not know how to interact with people in a way that would make them like me. An entire dorm now believed I was a violent freak. My ROTC platoon believed that I was a wimp and I could not even pass a PT test when they came around. When not being tested I could do it. When being tested I crumbled. I was a terrible cadet, and would have made a terrible soldier.

To add to the pain, sequestration hit. I was going to lose my three year scholarship because I had not secured it in time because I could not pass the PT test. Of course this added one more thing to my cycle of depression. I can't pass this stupidly easy PT test, so I am a failure. I am in danger of losing my scholarship and being cut from the program. I am a failure. Since I am going to lose the scholarship I will be placing a large financial burden on myself or my family. I am letting down my parents, the only people that still believe in me. I will be stealing my little sister's opportunities in the future because I am such a burden. I can't do that to her. I am a failure. I hate myself. I hate my life. Things would be so much easier if I could just stop existing. Life would be better if I were dead. The world would be better if I were dead. I hate myself. I wish I was dead.

I spent my November 4th, 18th birthday utterly alone. My family came down for lunch one day that week, but other than that I was utterly alone. Friends and family back home told me to "cheer up". No one could understand that I could not. I was berated on my birthday weekend by my parents and grandparents for being honest. I mentioned that I hated being here and being at Auburn. They told me to "cheer up" and that "you should be enjoying yourself, this is the best time in your life" and other things such as: "well if you would adjust your attitude, maybe you would find yourself enjoying this." I tried my damndest to improve my outlook, but I simply could not. The fact that I couldn't change myself when it appeared so easy for everyone else killed me. It was yet another thing that I was a failure at, yet another thing to pull me further into depression.

Over winter break, I simply worked and saw a few old

friends. Then we once again went our separate ways. They returned to college, and I sunk back deeper into my hell. For Valentine's Day I actually summoned my last ounces of courage, optimism and charisma and asked a girl out. She very surprisingly said yes. Valentine's Day rolled around and I was stood up. Not even a text or a phone call from her, she wouldn't answer any of mine either. I just stood waiting outside the restaurant for a good hour before I realized what was really happening. Just one more nail in the coffin.

My escape during this time was either to lie catatonically on my bed, or immerse myself in the video game Skyrim. In Skyrim I could have fun, explore the world, and have adventures. I was a hero. I had immense power. I could defeat the demons and dragons plaguing that virtual world. I wielded great swords to cut down these demons and dragons, I fought tooth and nail. I saved the world. I had grand adventures. No one in that single player virtual world judged me. I could act how I wanted. I was respected. Most importantly, I had fun. Unfortunately the fact that I spent more time in a virtual world than I did in class or interacting with people became apparent to me. I am a loser. I play this stupid video game all the time, and for what? Nothing. I get nothing out of this. It is a complete waste of my time. I am such a loser. I should get a life. This proves I don't have friends. I hate that I don't know how to make friends. I hate that I don't know how to meet girls. I hate myself for being this much of a loser. I am that freak that hides away in his room and plays video games all day. I am a loser. I hate myself and my miserable excuse for a life. Death sounds like a good solution. I hate that death sounds like a good solution. I hate myself for thinking this way... Depression had taken my last refuge and turned it against me. I literally had nothing to fall back on. My old friends were anywhere from 100-1000 miles away from me, and even then I am sure they were sick and tired of hearing me mope. Our relationships were deteriorating with time, distance, and my foul mood. They were all of enjoying their college experience, and here I was, trapped in some sort of hell unable to realize why I couldn't have the same experiences everyone else was. I thought that my old friends could easily live without me. I thought everyone would be better off without me. No one wanted to be around me when I was breathing, so obviously no one would care if I was dead.

I would lay there on my bed; maybe with music on, maybe with Netflix on. Sometimes I would have the lights on, most of the time I would stay in the dark. The music and Netflix were a vain attempt to mask the fact that I was laying there catatonically. The songs were all sad. The shows had no life. I heard them and they just helped add fuel to the fire. I never really watched the shows though; I never really listened to the songs. They were just background noise to the constant rush of thoughts in my head. The simple act of getting up from my bed to do anything was a struggle. Not a struggle with laziness, it was physically a struggle for me to move.

I would force myself to go and get food. It was painful for me to drag myself down four flights of stairs and to the dining hall that was only fifty yards outside my dorm's front door. I anguished over the interactions that I would be forced to have with the cooks, the cashier, someone I may run into. Every trip to get food might as well have been a journey to Middle Earth where I had to throw the one ring into the fires of Mount Doom. Some nights I could not bring myself to go get food. I just went hungry that night. It was easier for me. Every night I just lay there until it was time to go to sleep. Promptly at 9:00. Weekdays or weekends, I was in bed with the lights out by 9:00. It was the maximum amount of time I could deal with pretending to be alive. I did not sleep though, I would lay there some more, trapped in my head. Most weekends I would drive 100 miles home in a vain effort to escape myself. I learned rather quickly that my prison went with me wherever I went. It was inescapable.

Over Spring Break I had a small crack. I let it be known to my mom while with her on a mission trip to Honduras that I hated being in Army ROTC. That it was the reason that I "couldn't stop being so negative all the time." I was told to stop being negative for as long as I can remember. By my parents, by my grandparents, by friends, yet I could not make anyone understand that I simply couldn't stop. I figured I could act for a week. I love Honduras, and I love working with the kids in the orphanage where my family volunteers. I figured if I could act happy anywhere it could be here. Well, I am not that good of an actor. Yet I could not bring myself to spill it all to my mom. I tried to Band-Aid fix it. I told her I hated being in the Army and that I wanted out now. Since I had not accepted/ earned the scholarship I was ok by the Army to quit anytime I wanted. My mom promised me that it would be okay, and that through loans we could afford school. My parents would take on the loans. They assumed that once I was out of the Army that I would be happy again. I only wished that it was true.

Upon arriving back in Auburn I walked into the ROTC building and quit the Army. While I was never truly soldier material it was still something that I had wanted for a long time. Since childhood I wanted to serve in the military. Yet I quit. I was a failure. I had failed myself and made myself a further burden on my family. I had squandered a prime opportunity for a career and to have school paid for. I had failed everyone that ever wore a uniform. I couldn't even make it out of freshman year ROTC. I was ashamed to have ever told anyone that I was in the Army. I had let down my friends back home who were so excited when I came home and got to show off my ACU's. I let down myself. I am a failure. I hate myself for being a failure. I hate myself. I hate my life. I am not even worth the breath that I draw. I wish I wasn't here. I want to be dead. I should kill myself.

Nothing improved after I left ROTC. If anything it got worse. At least ROTC forced me to do things and interact with other people. I no longer had that. Depression had even taken my video game refuge from me. I was alone in the world. I was trapped. No physical locks or chains held me back, but I couldn't move. No one was physically abusing me, yet I was tortured constantly. It felt as if my very soul was tearing itself apart. I could not imagine myself having a future. I could not even imagine living through the next day. Every day was the worst day of my life, and I knew that no matter what, tomorrow would also be the worst day of my life, and the day after, and the day after. As a lay there in my catatonic state, only stirring to force myself to go to class, and sometimes not even then, I realized something. I realized that I had been fighting this for a long time. I realized that I had been fighting myself since 8th grade. At 18 years old I was tired of fighting. I wanted to escape. I did not want to keep on fighting. I could not keep on fighting. I was on the verge of giving up.

Naturally that made it worse on me. My desire to give up only succeeded in making me hate myself and devalue myself and my life more.

One night in mid-April. I went home for the weekend after class on Friday afternoon. I was home alone that Friday night for whatever reason. I was not in a good place, and suddenly I realized I had a way out. I could end my suffering.

On November 4th, 2012 I got "my own" handgun for my birthday. This was normal for me. I am an avid shooter and love shooting sports, plus I had been asking for a handgun for a long time. I am still very pro-gun rights and I love the 2nd Amendment. I have never raised a gun against a human being until that Friday night. My Smith and Wesson M&P 9mm is one of my most cherished possessions. I paid for part of it even though it was my birthday present. Technically my dad owns it, but on my 21st birthday it will legally become mine. My family considered it mine. Since I am in college and lived in a dorm on a gun-free campus, the gun would be kept at my family's home. The theory was that once I moved off campus I would get to keep it in my apartment for home defense. This night though, it was in my bedroom at home, right where I kept it.

I wanted an escape from my hell, and I finally found a key to the door. A 9mm 115-grain full metal jacket lead bullet that would be spat out of the end of my M&P 9 at around 1300 feet per second with the application of 5 pounds of pressure to the trigger. It would impact my brain before I had time to process any pain by unleashing approximately 570 joules of kinetic energy. Simple, effective, quick, and I could load and fire the gun in seconds. I had visualized my own death almost constantly for a few months now. This was the way I decided to go out. It was easy and it was quick. Shooting a gun was one of the last few things I actually thought I was any good at. I couldn't possibly screw it up. It was nearly impossible for my equipment to fail as I kept it in such a good condition. It was less risky than hanging, and quicker too. It was more certain than jumping off a building or bridge. It was faster than slitting my veins. I could control it more than overdosing or poison and it wouldn't give me time to regret my actions. I couldn't damn well miss, as the gun would be in contact with my head. A gun was an all or nothing solution. I had visualized all of these scenarios countless times, and with all of that in mind I opted to end my life and escape hell with a gun.

Reader. If you at all identify with this, whether it is the part about visualizing your death constantly, the self-hatred, or the desire to end your life please do yourself a favor and get help. If you are in the U.S. call 1-800-273-825, that number is for the National Suicide Hotline. I never gave it a call. I should have. I should have told someone. I should have mentioned how I felt to someone, anyone before it got this bad. The curse of depression was that I believed that I could not tell anyone, that even if I did it wouldn't matter anyway. Tomorrow was going to be the worst day of my life no matter what. I would wake up every day knowing it was going to be terrible and fall into a fitful sleep knowing tomorrow would bring the same. Reader, do not fall into that hole. It is a dark and scary place. It is hell. Reach out to someone. If you are a younger student, try a school counselor. Colleges have psychological services too. Seek help and save yourself. Don't let yourself get to the point that I am about to get to. I would look up at the night sky now and see blackness. I was reaching out for anything to hold on to in my life but I fell, and the stars that I had found so beautiful a few years ago were now black and cold to me. There was no way I could live like this anymore. I was at the edge of oblivion. I simply could not go on and continue fighting this losing battle.

I didn't want to live anymore. I was home alone. I had the means that I wanted to use to end my life. I walked into my bedroom, picked the gun case up from where it sat on the nightstand next to my bed. I opened it and took out my pistol. It was ice cold to the touch though the house is kept at 72 degrees. I sat down on the corner of my bed just holding the gun for a minute. I set it down. I picked up my laptop and I wrote a goodbye note. More specifically, a suicide note. In that note I spelled out to my family how I thought I was a burden and that I was miserable and how sorry I am that it came to this. I said goodbye to the friends that I thought might miss me; I confessed having feelings for a girl that I had liked since junior year of high school just so I could say I at least did that.

I confessed to my family that I did not believe I was going to heaven or hell because those places did not exist, and that I did not care. Death, even if after death it is only empty nothingness, it had to be better than this. I closed the laptop with the word document still open, made sure I had disabled my password, and set it on the bed next to me. My goodbyes sounded stupid. I could not effectively convey the deep love I felt for these people, my family, and my old friends. I found a sticky note and wrote "check the computer" on it and placed it on top of the closed laptop.

I returned my attention to the gun. I decided that if I was going to do this I was going to give myself a set time. This was meant so that I would hurry up and do it. I set my phone to play the song "Explorers" by Muse. It was either that song, or "Javert's Suicide" from my favorite play, Les Miserables. I opted for "Explorers" as I did not want to be that level of dramatic. "Explorers" is a beautifully sad song and although I do not listen to it much anymore, it is still a beautiful song. The lyrics of the chorus are: "free me, free me, free me from this world. I don't belong here, it was a mistake imprisoning my soul. Can you free me, free me from this world?" The entire song accurately portrayed how I felt inside. If you are reading this book as someone who is not depressed, I suggest you listen to it. Music is a universal language. That song might give you a small look into what I was feeling. Is the song actually about depression? No, as far as I can tell it is environmentalism and the destruction of our literal world. The beauty of music is that you can interpret it in any way you wish. A song that conjures up joy for some may bring sadness for others. I interpreted this one as a story of my life and my still as of yet unnamed and undiagnosed depression. It was a perfect representation of how I was feeling. It was the perfect song to end my life too.

The song lasts five minutes and forty six seconds. Five minutes and forty six seconds would be the time I gave myself to finish my miserable excuse for a life. If I could not do it in that time I was even more pathetic than I thought. I picked up the gun; it felt cold in my hands. I ejected the magazine that I knew to be empty and picked up the loaded magazine from the gun case. The magazine could hold seventeen bullets. I kept ten in there. I would only need one. As I slapped the magazine into the gun my heart began to beat faster and faster. I felt it up near my throat. I pressed play on the song. The musical countdown had begun.

I pulled back on the slide and let go, loading a round into the chamber. My gun has its' safety built into the trigger like a Glock, so it saved me a step. I was one motion of the arm and five pounds of pressure on the trigger using my index finger from being free. I brought my arm up. I began to cry. Not one or two tears. I was legitimately crying. I placed the gun against my temple. My hands were sweating. I was sweating all over. I felt the cold metal tip of the barrel against my now simultaneously hot and yet somehow clammy skin. I took a deep breath and cried some more. I moved the gun from my temple to my mouth. I quickly decided I did not like how that felt and moved it back to my temple. I lowered the gun and raised it a few more times. I realized the song was almost four minutes into it. I did not have long to go. I checked the chamber once again to make sure that I did in fact have a bullet in it. I would not want to successfully pull the trigger only to have the gun dry fire. I raised the gun one last time. I put it right back on my temple. "Explorers" entered its final swooping chorus. Through tears I choked out to the empty bedroom and to all the world, "goodbye." I closed my eyes and let out a tortured scream. Mentally I was pulling the trigger. I felt like I was throwing every ounce of strength into applying five pounds of pressure that I could, yet I could not finish pulling the trigger. I had depressed the trigger about halfway. Any second now I would finish the pull, firing the gun. I was screaming out loud at myself "do it! Come on you loser do it! Fuck, come on!" "Explorers" ended on its familiar soft notes. I had not done it. I had even failed at killing myself. I screamed again in frustration and anguish.

Knowing now that I was too weak to even kill myself, I rapidly unloaded the gun. I ejected the magazine, retracted the slide and ejected the bullet that did not have my name on it. I put the bullet back in the magazine. I put the empty magazine back in the gun, replaced the gun and its magazines in the case and slammed the lid shut. I put it back in its normal spot. I opened the laptop and deleted my suicide note. I then lay on my bed and broke down and sobbed. I could still feel where the gun had been placed against my head. To this day I can still feel the cold metal against my temple.

CHAPTER 11
"BACK UP TO THE SHINING WORLD"

This was now a Saturday. I felt worse than usual. The reality of what I had seriously tried to do that night had set in. I had succeeded in terrifying myself. I knew that I did not want to live in the world of mental anguish that I had inhabited for so long anymore. I still wanted to escape. I guess I had cried myself to sleep that night, I don't really remember. I woke up the next morning, went downstairs and just sat at the kitchen table. Trying to be as casual as possible I got up, got breakfast, and sat back down. I didn't touch it. My dad asked if I could help him with yard work. To keep the façade of normality, I agreed to help in the yard. He went ahead to get started working while I was supposed to finish my breakfast. I sat there at the kitchen table in sullen silence. My mom, who must have noticed something off about me that day, roused me from silence and asked me a simple "what's up?" I held off the questioning for a minute or two. I was just "zoning out" and I "didn't get a good night's sleep." Both were true, just not the whole truth. My mom could tell there was something more than that. I tried to get up to leave and go help my dad with the yard work. She grabbed my arm and asked me what was really wrong. I sat back down and broke down crying. I said nothing. She must have been confused by my sudden breakdown and continued asking what was wrong and if I was okay. This was the hardest moment in my life, and I couldn't get out of it. No amount of persuasive power or crafty words would have convinced my mother to let me leave that table in tears without giving an inkling of what was wrong. I was truthfully very scared. I had to look at the person who had brought me into this world and tell her that I hated myself and hated life so bad that I had tried to kill myself.

I had just finished telling all of this to my mom when my dad came back inside the house to try and hurry me along with breakfast since he did not want us outside doing yardwork during the heat of the day. Instead of his son sitting at the table taking his sweet time to eat, he found me and my mom both in tears. My mom was giving me a hug and refusing to let go. My dad was concerned and began asking what was going on. I had to tell my dad the same story I had just finished telling my mom. It was no easier to tell my story to him. If anything it was harder. I was always worried about disappointing my dad. My dad had sacrificed a lot for me over the years. Everything from taking time to be an adult leader when I was a Boy Scout, to helping me learn to drive, to playing with Lego blocks when I was a small child, to taking a job in another state so I could afford to stay at school. I looked up to him long before I realized the sheer amount he did for me. I have never wanted to disappoint him and always strived to avoid doing that. When he hugged me after I told him my story and joined my mother in promising that everything would be fine and that we would work through this, it was a huge moment of relief. I had reached the bottom of hell, and after a considerably long and terrible stay there I was finally on the path to climb out the other side.

The next few weeks were a whirlwind. That Monday my mom made an appointment with my general care doctor. The doctor sent me to a psychologist in Birmingham and prescribed anti-depressants. I was officially diagnosed with depression. That was an easy diagnosis. I had a mindset change rather quickly following my final fall apart; I still wanted to get rid of myself, but just in a different way. I tried to change who I was. The easiest way I thought for me to do that was to change my major. By changing my major I must have thought that I would put myself on an entirely new path vastly different from the "old me." I switched majors from history to business. I had a desire to get better and see my mental health improve. I was tired of feeling depressed. I found some fight left in me after all. It would be a long climb that was not without its slips and falls. I had a long journey ahead of me, but I was finally on my way out of hell.

I went through that summer working a part time job, and working on myself. I was not going to let this next year of college be ruined by what I now knew was depression. I was bound and determined that this year would be different. I was legitimately excited for sophomore year of college to start. I had set it up so that I would be rooming with a great friend that I knew from high school and Boy Scouts who was in the grade below me. I would also be rooming with two other people because we had a suite. One I kind of knew as an acquaintance and the other whom I did not know at all. We were all from the same city so we got together over summer and talked about the next year. We all got along great and the year started off on a good note.

Almost a week into the year I was already bored of sitting in my room and determined not to let my boredom become a catalyst for the resurgence of my depression. So I was browsing the Auburn University groups, clubs, and activities website and one thing jumped out at me. It was a "Coed Service fraternity founded on the principals of Boy Scouts." Its name was Alpha Phi Omega. Being an Eagle Scout myself I found myself more than mildly interested. I was thrown off a bit by the Greek letters attached to the group. The word "fraternity" also had a very negative connotation in my mind. I had no good experiences with anything Greek letter. I assumed sorority girls looked down on me because I was not in a frat, and frat guys looked down on me because I was also not in a frat and did not dress or act like them. Plus my roommate freshman year had firmly cemented the negative definition of "frat" or "Greek" in my head. For this I owe the Greek community and apology, while there is some truth to the stereotype…a lot of people that I now know in Greek organizations are actually pretty great people.

So I decided what the hell, I was going to rush this strange fraternity that was apparently coed, had no house, and was based on Scouting principals and was a "Service Fraternity" whatever the hell that meant. It sounded weird in the best way possible. This type of weird is right up my alley. I went to the first rush event: "Meet the Brothers and play a game of ultimate Frisbee!" My senior year in high school, especially second semester once all my responsibilities calmed down, all I did was play Frisbee. I was actually pretty good at Frisbee if I don't say so myself. This event was tailor made for me to show off.

I went, met the Brothers (there were three females and yes, they are called Brothers too.) Despite me being the ultimate try-hard at a friendly game of Frisbee, I apparently made a good enough impression (and a helluva diving catch to score in the game) that they invited me back to all the other rush events. Two community service projects, and a bowling event.

I went to the two projects, but could not make the bowling event. From there a brother texted me and invited to "Formal Rush" where I may or may not receive a bid to pledge Delta Chapter of Alpha Phi Omega. There were no guarantees I would be let in to pledge. I showed up to Formal Rush in the "Eagle's Nest." The Eagle's Nest is a large conference and event room at the top of the Haley Center, the tallest building on Auburn's campus at a whopping 9 stories. It is also the tallest building in the entire county just in case you were wondering. I was more than a little nervous at the prospect of being actively judged on if I was allowed to stick around or not.

After a while of mingling and small talk with the brothers and other potential pledges, one of the female brothers pulled me aside and handed me this small notecard with a really intricate printed coat of arms on one side, and a Greek letter delta on the other. She then said: "I formally invite you to pledge Delta Chapter of Alpha Phi Omega, inside this letter are instructions to show up next week on Thursday at 5:00 PM at Ross Square Fountain, be wearing full formal attire. Do not be late." I was in. Well, I was in as a pledge, but still. I was in and in the moment that was good enough for me.

Freshman year I would never have even dreamed of talking to these people, much less ever thinking about trying to gain entrance to their fraternity. I was shocking myself, my family, and my friends back home. I chalk this all up to my willpower to recover. I wanted to get better; I did not want to let depression rule my life, so with the help of medication I was making great strides towards making my life more "normal". For the first time in a long time I started to feel a real sense of optimism about the future.

I showed up at Ross Square Fountain at the appropriate date and time and wearing the appropriate attire. It was there that I first met my soon to be pledge brothers. Less than an hour later we were officially pledges. We even had a pledge pin and pledge manual. There were seven of us at the Fountain, only one girl, and one more pledge would join us the next week. He had work at the time and simply could not get off work. Two of my fellow pledges decided almost immediately that this was not for them. A guy and a girl dropped within a week of each other. This was week two of our ten week pledge period. Over the next eight weeks I would become closer to these guys and the brothers faster than I thought possible. We had tailgates, went to football games together, did many service projects together, hung out on the weekends, had parties, and did normal college things. It felt amazing to be part of a group that genuinely wanted me around. Whether it be meeting up with as many people from the fraternity as possible for "Monday Moe's" or just seeing each other on campus and stopping to have a conversation. This was a complete 180 from how I was acting at this time freshman year.

About two weeks into the pledge process you are assigned a "Big Brother". A Big Brother is supposed to guide you through you pledge period and help you learn about the chapter and what it takes to actually initiate. As a pledge you are allowed to submit your requests for a Big Brother. I really did not want one of the female brothers to be my Big Brother because this is a fraternity and I was dead set that a fraternity should be only for guys. Still, my third choice was one of the female brothers. Here we are just going to call her "S". Well it came time for us to find out who we got, the brothers had us meet at Ross Square Fountain in suits and we went from there. By the time it was all over I knew that my Big Brother was "S". I'll admit to being slightly disappointed at first, but the second she was allowed to talk to me my disappointment vanished. S told me how when the brothers were deciding who got which pledge, she demanded that she have me as her Little Brother. That was flattering. S and I would become the best of friends over the next eight weeks. As we got to know each other she told me her demons, some of which make my depression look like child's play… I told her mine. We understood each other. We became great friends. We did what the Big Brother/ Little Brother program is really supposed to do. Somehow I am supposed to be a bridesmaid at her wedding. Bridesman? Whatever the word is, I am absolutely not wearing a dress.

While my pledging period was fun, it was also challenging. I had 14 multi-faceted pledge requirements that I had to complete before they would allow me to initiate, or rather before they would allow us to initiate. We were told that "we only initiate pledge classes, not individual pledges." This required that I become even closer to my five pledge brothers.

We gave ourselves the nickname "The Sexy Six" and charged on towards what we hoped would be initiation providing none of us got dropped. We refused to let anyone else quit. One of us tried, but we convinced him to stay. "Fabulous Five" just does not sound awesome... we had to stay the Sexy Six.

Together we learned what it means to be a Brother of Alpha Phi Omega in Delta Chapter. Together my pledge class and I overcame a whole lot of challenges, and towards the end of our pledge period we got to vote amongst ourselves who would get the "Most Outstanding Pledge Award." This award would be presented by the Brothers to a pledge towards the very end of the pledge period at the same time the pledges presented a Brother with the "Most Outstanding Brother Award." Well to cap off this Cinderella story of my turnaround, I was elected by my pledge brothers as Most Outstanding Pledge. My award was a paddle made by the previous Outstanding Pledge specifically for me. The previous Outstanding Pledge presented me with my very own Outstanding Pledge paddle as tradition stated.

Immediately upon leaving the banquet my pledge brothers took my paddle to "have a look at it." Before I knew it they were chasing me around the parking lot of a really nice restaurant trying to paddle me with it. It was all in good fun, and I got them back, some would go on to become "Outstanding Brother" in their own right and be presented with their own paddle. You had better believe I chased them around with their paddle.

On November 10th 2013, in the wee hours of the morning, I was initiated and became a Brother of Delta Chapter of Alpha Phi Omega. I had earned this.. I earned it with help from the brothers, from S, and from my pledge brothers. I have done a few things that I am proud of in my life, this is easily the proudest I had been of myself in a long time. I came from this time last year alone; miserable, not wanting to live, to now. Like that scene towards the end of "Indiana Jones and the Last Crusade" I had stepped out into the canyon, trusting the words of others that an invisible bridge was there. To my great rejoicing my feet touched solid ground and I walked continued walking forward.

So reader, if you identified with me at any point during the *long dark sad parts of this book, I want you to know that it can get better. It takes a lot. You have to be willing to fight back. I don't know you, and I may never, but if I can fight back against my depression, <u>so can you</u>. If you have any sort of mental affliction, I know you can fight back. It is going to be hard, and no one will understand just how hard it is but you, yet trust me. The fight might be hard but <u>it is entirely worth it.</u>*

Now, I am not saying my recovery was without setbacks. In fact, I even had a relapse. During and after winter break a pervasive feeling of unhappiness crept in again. It actually had no reason to, I thought I was good, I was on medication and I had just achieved a great goal. I slowly began to realize that the really low dose of medication was only holding my depression at bay, and that my recovery was not going to be as easy as I had thought.

The same old patterns started happening as I lost my footing. I became incredibly stressed over my academic performance. My grades were not very good. I was discovering that balancing an active social life with schoolwork and sleep is tough. Not to mention I was quickly disenchanted with my decision to switch majors and join the business school. Numbers, economics, numbers, calculus, numbers…none of this stuff really excites me and it was apparent in my work. My grades were poor as a result of my lack of effort in school and my overzealousness in my social life. Fear of failure has always held me back, and I was quite literally failing now. Depression crept back in. My mindset deteriorated, and I caught myself visualizing my death more often than not. I quickly lost all hope. I gave up so fast that I am ashamed of how easy I let all of my progress slip. My thoughts turned fatalistic. If my life was doomed to go back into depression constantly then I did not want to live anymore. If I was doomed to be miserable my entire life, then why continue life if I couldn't truly be alive?

Thankfully I did not let myself go too far. I quickly realized that the depression had begun to take over and that my death desire was not how I actually felt. I did not totally give up. I realized that I just needed to keep fighting. This time though, I decided to take off immediately and nuke the site from orbit. It was the only way to be sure… Aliens' references aside, I did take the "nuclear" option immediately. I decided to talk to my parents and try and get out in front of this problem. I also changed my major from business back to history, my GPA thanked me.

Naturally my relapse worried my mom and dad, it worried me too. Thankfully, they got me more help and fast. After my lackluster experience with my first psychologist I was incredibly skeptical about going to see another one. I know I did want to see about getting my medication dosage increased though. Even I could see that my depression rated more than the lowest dose possible.

So with some convincing I made an appointment to go to Auburn University's Counseling Center. To me, the big attraction was that it was "free" to students. It had already been paid for it in the cost of tuition. So even if it turned out that talking to a psychologist wasn't for me, then at least my family would not be out a ridiculous sum of money. I can't put a price on mental health, but at $120 for a 50 minute session where nothing really happened and I was not helped at all…I can definitely say it is not worth that, and I am sort of appalled at the high cost of mental healthcare. Heck all healthcare in general. I don't know the root cause and do not claim to be an expert at all on healthcare or healthcare reform, but I do know that it is expensive and that cost is felt by us, the consumers, I was just happy to find something "free." It made the risk-reward calculation easier. I guess I did manage to learn something in economics class.

So I went to the Student Counseling Services (from here on abbreviated SCS) with a lot of skepticism. I got there and it was a typical psychologist waiting room: the warm lighting, soft music, posters everywhere about combatting different issues. Nothing too fancy, but it wasn't bad and served its purpose. The receptionist took me to a bank of computers where I was administrated the "entrance" exam. I am not sure what the technical psychological term for it is, but I know I had taken something similar the first time I saw a psychologist. The first time I took the test I did not feel the test was comprehensive enough and asked much more vague questions. This test was point blank. It straight up asked me to rate my desire to live. It asked me to rate how I felt on a daily basis. This test helped show the SCS that I had a few immediate problems to work on.

From there I was handed off to a psychologist. Immediately I could tell it was going to go better than my previous experience with a psychologist. This guy, we will call him "D", was incredibly concerned with my well-being right from the get go. The best part was that his concern felt genuine. He outlined how he tries to run his sessions: he realizes at first that he is probably going to be doing most of the talking, but as we progress he wanted me to take over the talking. His main goals were to help me identify the underlying problems, and find a way to rework my thought process to stop what I referred to in this book as a "deluge" or "torrent" of depressive thoughts. He told me that the road would be tough, but that it was doable. It was his job to give me the support required to help me through this, but ultimately it would be up to me to help myself.

In my second session I opened up more. I related my entire story to him just as I have to you. I expressed to him my desires. That I wanted to feel "normal". That I wanted to experience good days along bad. That I was tired of being alone in the shadows of my mind. That I wanted to live and that I wanted to experience life as fully as I could. So that is what I did. With bi-weekly counseling, and an increase in my dosage of medication I realized that living was possible.

I am writing this book at the closing of my sophomore year. I am 19 and a half years old. For a person who did not even want to see 19 when they were turning 18, that is a huge accomplishment. I am in a fraternity. My grades are pretty good and I have changed my major back to my passion of history. I work out as often as possible except when I shirk gym time to write this book or a few other books I am working on. I hang out with friends if not on a daily basis, then at least multiple times a week. I have written the majority of this book in public. I sat in the Student Center and just wrote, in front of any number of people who decided to be in there that day. Last year, I would not have dreamed of being out in public for any amount of time. On nice days I can often be found in a hammock with sweet tea and either my laptop to write with/watch Netflix on, or a good book to read.

I have had one relationship this year. It was pretty short, and when it ended I was okay. Yeah it sucked in the moment, but I knew that life would go on. I have wrecked on my motorcycle, healed myself and rebuilt the bike. I have a social life, I go out in public, and I enjoy being outside again. My accomplishments this year may not sound like a lot to some of you, in fact it sounds sort of like a normal life. To me, that is a massive improvement. Now when I am in my room alone and don't want to be, I find something to do. I call up my friends and see if they can hang out. If for whatever reason they can't hang out I find something to do to entertain myself, whether it be forcing myself to study, or simply walking around and enjoying this beautiful campus and town.

I have noticed my ability to enjoy the "little things" has increased. I know that sounds cheesy, but it is true. When I was in the throes of my depression I could not enjoy anything. The world had lost its shine. The colors were no longer vibrant. The food did not taste as good. Every kind gesture someone gave me I turned it away. Now, I catch myself every now and then noticing the little things. Sweet tea tastes sweeter, and I can feel the warmth of the sunshine. The world is brighter to me now.

To use a metaphor: depression is like a pair of eye glasses. Eye glasses are supposed to be made of clear glass so that the wearer can see everything: the darkness, the light, the blues, the reds, everything. Depression is like wearing glasses with the lenses made of obsidian. For those that haven't had many geology courses: obsidian is a volcanic rock that is termed "volcanic glass". While it looks and feels like glass, it has one distinct difference from glass. Obsidian is jet black. Obsidian is nigh impossible to see through. With obsidian glasses on, that is all the wearer would see: darkness. The entire world would be dark. Beautiful and amazing things could be going on right before the wearer's eyes, but the obsidian would block it from view. The wearer might have friends and loved ones all around, and they could be experiencing incredible things, but they would not know it. The obsidian would block their view. The worst part is, very few people can understand that your glasses are made of obsidian. They feel that your glasses are clear like theirs, and that you must just be "having a bad day," or that you should really "stop being negative all the time." Now, I feel like I am living without the obsidian glasses on.

CHAPTER 12
FOUR YEARS LATER: "AND ONCE MORE SAW THE STARS"

It has been over four years since I first published *Hell Has No Stars*. A whole lot has gone on in those four years, so much that I felt it worthwhile to revisit this book. My final two years of college were overall pretty great. I did have some mental health setbacks of course, yet every time I rallied and continued pushing forward. The road was not easy, but I have so far found a way to overcome and persevere. I have changed medications twice in that time frame. One of them made me not feel depressed, but also managed to make me feel nothing at all. For all the modern fascination with the zombie apocalypse with shows like "The Walking Dead", it is no fun being a non-feeling zombie. It took me a while to figure out how poorly those meds were making me feel...or rather not feel. Thankfully I have since switched off of those meds and am now on one that I feel is working incredibly for me.

Those final two years in college I managed to keep my desire to help bring about positive change in relation to mental health alive. My counselor from the SCS, "D", helped introduce me to a club on campus called Active Minds. Active Minds is a national organization that is focused on changing the conversation about mental health to end the stigma. While the organization primarily makes its home in chapters at hundreds of colleges and universities across the country, Active Minds' mission allows it to serve everyone in a community. I became involved with Auburn University's chapter of Active Minds in my junior year. With the help of "D" to setup the occasion, the Auburn chapter asked me to come speak about my then newly published book and my struggle with depression. It was my first public speaking event on the subject. I thought I did alright. They even had a reporter from the school newspaper and a camera team from the school TV channel. I met with the President and founder of Auburn's Active Minds chapter after I gave my talk. He was a senior at that point and had founded the Auburn University chapter because he had suffered the loss of a good friend to suicide.

He used his grief and pain that he felt at the loss of his friend to try and make a difference. I would soon learn that most people involved with our local Active Minds chapter had similar stories and all of them truly believed in the fight to end the stigma around mental illness. That year we held an "Out of the Darkness" walk in cooperation with the American Foundation for Suicide Prevention. AFSP helps run suicide prevention hotline call centers, works with the families that have suffered a loss to suicide and many other great causes. Our chapter was nominated for an award from Auburn University that year. Sadly we as an organization would not receive an award. Our President and founder however would receive the Outstanding Male Student of the Year award. In my opinion he thoroughly deserved it.

I was still involved with Alpha Phi Omega and during that time I made the rounds of a few leadership positions. I thought I was growing weary of being involved with the fraternity and was planning to sit out my senior year and focus on Active Minds and the very important detail of actually trying to graduate. Senior year rolls around and I was elected as the Vice President of Active Minds. My fraternity also chose to name me as Pledge Trainer, leaving me in charge of molding a pledge class from being a bunch of individuals to a united group that would be almost like family. I could not pass up the opportunity to take on the responsibility of Pledge Trainer. Classes were also picking up in intensity since I was a senior. I did a lot of writing that year, most of it in the form of historical research papers. Somehow I also had time for an internship at a local Civil War museum.

That fall semester, Active Minds once again worked with AFSP to put on the "Out of the Darkness" walk. This time I was helping organize it since I was Vice President. Credit to the Active Minds president. She had enormous shoes to fill after the graduation of the last president and founder. She did an incredible job. Together with the rest of our executive staff and numerous volunteers the Out of the Darkness walk raised almost $25,000 for AFSP. It was an incredible moment.

That year Auburn's "Miss Homecoming" ran for her position on a mental health/end the stigma platform. She was a member of Active Minds and asked us for help with her

campaign since it worked towards a common cause. All the
Miss Homecoming candidates have "platforms" and they are
given access to funds to help see out their platform. As part of
her campaign I was asked to share my story to a large
audience of a bunch of complete strangers whom I never really
thought of associating with. Naturally Miss Homecoming
candidates hold events at places that can summon large voting
blocs such as fraternities and sororities, and often the
candidates themselves are from sororities. I had not cared
about the competition until that year. Yet here I was, standing
in front of an amphitheater filled with the frattiest frat bros and
sorority girls on a panel of five people that all shared our
stories. In the end, our candidate won her election. As part of
her campaign promises she helped put together for the second
year running a "mental wealth week" on campus. It was put
together by her campaign, Active Minds, and some of the
previously mentioned top tier frat bros and their fraternity who
felt called to action. It was pleasant to have a large incredibly
diverse group of people coming together to make a difference
for mental health.

At that point I was nearing graduation .I was wrapping up
my senior thesis and my internship at the National Civil War
Naval Museum in Columbus, Georgia had already drawn to a
close. I had begun looking for jobs after graduation. It was
around this time that I decided to take my book off of the
proverbial shelf. My original thinking was to edit it and put it
back up as soon as I could. Yet once it was down I had a
change of heart. I thought that I was closing the book on this
chapter of my life. I was not doing much with the book and
did not plan on making a career with it. I still don't. I just
assumed that when I graduated college that my avenues for
mental health advocacy would dry up.

With the book down, and graduation rapidly approaching I
applied for jobs almost everywhere. From automobile related
businesses to the National Parks Service. From the Alabama
State Historical Archives to heavy industry sales
representative. I graduated in May 2016 from Auburn
University with a Bachelor's Degree in History. Unfortunately
I did not hear back from any of the jobs I applied to and ended

up moving home and taking a part time job. After about a week of being the lowest person on the totem pole in a department store and living at home after years of freedom...I knew I needed to do something different. I had always known deep down that I wanted to teach history, yet I was not qualified to teach in the United States. So I began looking outside the US to find a teaching opportunity, even if it was only volunteer.

I wound up on the tiny but beautiful island territory of American Samoa teaching 7th grade science and 5th grade everything in an elementary school. American Samoa is owned by the US, but is in such desperate need for teachers that they were willing to take me on. It was a massive learning experience for me. I learned that I had absolutely zero idea how to teach, run a classroom, open a coconut, or about anything else. 8,000 miles away from home is a long way away to figure this stuff out. I wound up getting a massive infection and returning to Alabama. American Samoa is a beautiful place with many friendly people and a unique culture. My students, while rowdy and nigh uncontrollable at times helped me figure out what I want to do with life. The very few moments of clarity in the classroom, where my lesson made sense and I could see the students lighting up as they figured things out made it worth it. I only wish that I knew how to be a proper teacher so that I could have taught those kids better and done a better service for them.

This leads me to today. Upon arriving home I applied for graduate school back at Auburn University. Coincidentally Auburn has a great Social Science Education department and I was familiar with the town and still had friends in the area. I was accepted and I find myself there now learning how to be actually teach. I am back involved with Active Minds again, and it was there that I ran into "D" again. He asked me if I had any plans to republish my book. Being a mental health advocate never left me. In American Samoa I saw just how far, we here on the mainland, have come with regards to mental health advocacy. While in American Samoa, I did my best to help my students. It was hard hearing from some of them how they were bullied, especially since as a teacher I was supposed to be a neutral arbiter. My mental health also struggled over there. Between being 8,000 miles from everything I have ever really known and the stress of trying to be an effective teacher with zero idea what I was doing, my mental health slipped again. It helped me remember that my fight is never truly over, on a personal level and reaching out to help others. So here I am, four years later. Life is not a fairy tale and it never will be. Yet in five years I have made a comeback from the brink of my own destruction to living a fairly normal, happy and fulfilling life. I am excited to see how my journey continues.

Reader, I thank you for following along with me through my trials and tribulations and finally my fight back. If this book helps one person in some way that I do not even realize, I would be thrilled. Reader, I encourage you to continue the fight back. Fight back. If it is for your own mental health or for someone you love. Even if you have been fortunate enough to not be affected in anyway by mental health issues, I still encourage you to help fight back. Seek help if you need it. It is out there, <u>do not believe the stigma. You can beat it. I know that together we can change the stigma so that in the future others will not have to suffer.</u>

*"To get back up to the shining world from there
My guide and I went into that hidden tunnel,*

*And Following its path, we took no care
To rest, but climbed: he first, then I-so far,
through a round aperture I saw appear*

*Some of the beautiful things that Heaven bears,
Where we came forth, and once more saw the stars."*
-Dante Alighieri, *Inferno*

Need help? In the U.S., call 1-800-273-TALK (8255)
National Suicide Prevention Lifeline
www.suicidepreventionlifeline.org

ACKNOWLEDGMENTS

To my Mom and Dad: thank you for helping me through the dark, and for being the most supportive parents for my whole life.

To my friends: who have been there since the beginning, through the darkness, and forward unto dawn. I would not be here without you.

To my Fraternity Brothers: for helping me to gain the confidence to write this book, and being supportive of me in my endeavors.

To "D": thank you for loving your job as a psychologist, and your earnest desire to help people like me heal our mental scars and gain control of our minds. You were a major help to me.

To the many great people working towards a greater future for all who struggle with mental health issues that I have been fortunate enough to meet. It is their work and my desire to continue the fight that inspired me to edit and republish this work. Thank you.

Finally, to you Reader, thank you for giving my book I read. No matter your reason for reading, I hope you have found what you were looking for and that you have a long and prosperous life.

LEARN MORE ABOUT THE AUTHOR

You can follow Justin or leave a comment or review at:

www.amazon.com/author/JustinAMercer

www.facebook.com/JustinAMercer

41844877R10046